Behind
the Net

Behind
the Net

101 Incredible Hockey Stories

STAN FISCHLER

SPORTS
PUBLISHING

Sports Publishing books may be purchased in bulk at special discounts
for sales promotion, corporate gifts, fund-raising, or educational purposes.
Special editions can also be created to specifications. For details, contact
the Special Sales Department, Sports Publishing,
307 West 36th Street, 11th Floor, New York, NY 10018 or
sportspubbooks@skyhorsepublishing.com.

Sports Publishing® is a registered trademark of
Skyhorse Publishing, Inc.®, a Delaware corporation.

Visit our website at www.sportspubbooks.com.

10 9 8 7 6 5 4 3 2 1

Library of Congress Cataloging-in-Publication Data is available on file.

ISBN: 978-1-61321-414-5

Printed in the United States of America

Contents

Acknowledgements   ix

Foreword   xi

I Hockey History

1. TORONTO'S "DREADED" THREE-GOAL LEAD   2
2. THE SECOND-LONGEST GAME   5
3. HOW HOCKEY'S FIRST MAJOR STRIKE LED TO NEW YORK GETTING ITS FIRST NHL TEAM   11
4. THE NHL'S MOST INCREDIBLE FIGHT   13
5. THE BOOTLEGGER AND THE BODYCHECKERS   18
6. THE NIGHT THE RANGERS GOT TALKED OUT OF A PLAYOFF BERTH   21
7. HOCKEY'S AMAZING BROTHER ACTS   24
8. THE OTHER OLYMPIC MIRACLE, IN 1960   27
9. A BROTHERLY BROADCASTING TRIFECTA   32
10. HOW UNCLE SAM BEAT JOHNNY CANUCK TO PRO HOCKEY   33
11. THE "PERFECT" GOALIE IS A HOAX   34
12. HOW TO BECOME A TRAINER BY WALKING DOWN THE STREET   36
13. WHY JOINING A UNION ONCE WAS DANGEROUS FOR HOCKEY PLAYERS   38
14. HOW A DETROIT FAN TURNED A LIVE OCTOPUS INTO A WINNING TEAM'S SYMBOL   40
15. BABE RUTH, BUCK AND FRANK BOUCHER   42
16. THE OTHER STANLEY CUP   44
17. THE RICHARD RIOT   46
18. FIRST GOALIE TO USE A WATER BOTTLE   49
19. HOW THE ELEPHANTS BEAT THE RANGERS—THREE IN A ROW   50
20. HOW THE RANGERS TEASED GORDIE HOWE OFF THE TEAM   53
21. WORLD HOCKEY ASSOCIATION—THE LITTLE LEAGUE THAT COULD, ALMOST   55
22. THE STRANGE TRAVELS OF THE STANLEY CUP   59
23. HOW THE DUCKS CREATED AN NHL TEAM ON LONG ISLAND   63

24. HOW A WALK AROUND THE BLOCK SAVED THE ISLANDERS FRANCHISE   66

25. SANTA'S FAVORITE HOCKEY TEAM   68

II Colorful Characters

26. THE SWEET ALL-AMERICA "DOCTOR" TURNS SOUR GOON   72

27. HOW AN NHL PLAYER CREATED A NEW RULE   76

28. HOW TO TURN SUPERSTITIONS INTO A WIN   78

29. THE GAYE STEWART KISS IN THE GARDEN   79

30. PETTY CASH   80

31. HOW LYNN PATRICK REGAINED A ROSTER SPOT WHEN HIS FATHER, THE G.M., SAID NO   83

32. HOW A BULLET BECOMES A CORKSCREW IN ONE EASY LESSON   85

33. TURNABOUT IS FAIR PLAY   86

34. FROM THE PENALTY BOX TO THE PULPIT   88

35. HAP DAY AND WALTER PRATT   91

36. HOW CHING JOHNSON WAS UN-AMERICAN TO THE AMERICANS   94

37. THE HOCKEY PLAYER WHO SERVED AS THE TEAM CLOWN   96

38. THE HOCKEY-INTENSE MAYOR OF NEW YORK CITY   98

39. HOCKEY ORGANISTS ARE PART OF THE FUN   99

40. MARCEL PRONOVOST—THE MOST EMBROIDERED MAN IN HOCKEY   101

41. THE MOST TRAVELED STICKHANDLER   103

III Unlikely Heroes

42. A ONE-EYED REFEREE BECOMES A HALL OF FAMER   108

43. RED BERENSON—FROM OBSCURITY TO STARDOM IN ONE EASY SIX-GOAL GAME   112

44. BILL STEWART—BASEBALL UMPIRE BECOMES BLACKHAWKS COACH; AND WINS A CUP   113

45. MALIK ENDS NHL'S LONGEST SHOOTOUT   115

46. COYOTES PLUCK AMATEUR GOALIE TO SERVE AS BACKUP AFTER ILYA
    BRYZGALOV FALLS ILL   117

47. HOW A BUSHER WON THE LONGEST PLAYOFF GAME   120

48. THE TOTALLY IMPROBABLE DEVILS 1988 PLAYOFF RUN   126

49. THE MYSTERY NHL CAMEO APPEARANCE OF LARRY KWONG   128

50. THERE IS A TAVERN—AND A GOALIE—IN THE TOWN(Alfie Moore) 132
51. MIRACLE MYLES 135
52. HOW ONE OF HOCKEY'S GREATEST STARS WAS DISCOVERED ON THE FOOTBALL FIELD 137
53. JOE MILLER—A JOKE BOOK AND A GOALIE 139
54. THE MOST TOTALLY IMPROBABLE TWO-GOALIE ROTATION 141
55. HOW THE SKINNIEST GUY BECAME A TOP SCORER 142
56. PUNCH IMLACH'S IMPROBABLE PLAYOFF CRUSADE 145
57. HOW MICKEY MOUSE BECAME A RALLYING CRY FOR THE DEVILS FRANCHISE 149

IV Incredible Feats/Personalities

58. HOW A LONG-SHOT HORSE BET TURNED TORONTO INTO A WINNING TEAM 154
59. THE ULTIMATE CASE OF RUBBER-ITIS—AND AN INCREDIBLE SAVE AT SEA 157
60. THEY SAID IT COULDN'T BE DONE AND YET IT WAS DONE—BUT ONLY ONCE! 159
61. HE SCORED A GOAL, BUT NOT WITH HIS STICK: HOW COME? 163
62. HOW "THE CAPTAIN" DELIVERED ON HIS GUARANTEE 165
63. THE IMPOSSIBLE ONE-MAN SCORING SPURT—THREE GOALS IN 21 SECONDS 167
64. HOCKEY FIRST, SLEEP LATER 169
65. HATS OFF, DEREK!—HOW A ROOKIE DID THE IMPOSSIBLE IN HIS NHL DEBUT 170
66. RED KELLY—THE MOST ASTONISHING TRANSFORMATION 172
67. LEO REISE, JR.: A DEFENSEMAN WITH A STRATEGIC OFFENSE 174
68. SOMEONE WHO ACTUALLY PLAYED FOR SEVERAL HOCKEY TEAMS,
    A BASKETBALL CLUB, AND THE BROOKLYN DODGERS 176
69. DON'T MESS WITH THE ROCKET 178
70. ART COULTER: A HERO FOR THE RANGERS—A HERO FOR THE COAST GUARD 180
71. A RECORD THAT CAN NEVER—EVER—BE BROKEN, THANKS TO BUTCH GORING 181
72. THE COACH WITH A TRIFECTA OF CHAMPIONSHIPS—GENTLEMAN JOE PRIMEAU 183
73. FROM STAIRWAY TO STARDOM 185
74. STAAL, STAAL, AND STAAL 186
75. WHO'S MEL HILL? CHECK OUT "SUDDEN DEATH," AND YOU'LL FIND OUT! 188
76. NOT ONLY THE GREATEST, BUT THE ONLY AMBIDEXTROUS SUPERSTAR SCORER 191
77. CHARLIE GARDINER—A STUDY IN COURAGE BEYOND THE CALL OF DUTY 192

78. HOW PENTTI LUND EXTINGUISHED THE ROCKET'S RED GLARE   195

79. THE UN-MASKED GOALIE AND HIS AMAZING RECORD   198

80. THE MOST STITCHED-UP PLAYER IN HOCKEY WAS ALSO ONE OF THE BEST   201

81. ONE WINNING GOAL PICTURED TWO DIFFERENT WAYS   203

V Outrageous

82. HOW THE RANGERS PULLED A RE-NAMING FLIMFLAM FOR AN ENTIRE SEASON   206

83. THE RED WING WHO "COULDN'T" SHOOT THE PUCK IN THE OCEAN   209

84. THE LINESMAN WHO NEVER FORGOT THAT HE WAS A HALL OF FAME HITTER   212

85. WHEN THE MOB NEARLY MAULED A GOALIE   214

86. HOW A LIVE GOOSE VETOED A LIVE NHL PRESIDENT   218

87. BY DOGSLED TO THE STANLEY CUP FINAL   222

88. THE LIVE SKATING BEAR ON HOCKEY ICE   224

89. IF THE NAME IS TOO LONG – CHANGE IT!   228

90. WHEN TWO WRONG GIACOMINS MAKE A RIGHT   229

91. "KILL THE REFEREE!"—THIS TIME IT NEARLY HAPPENED   231

92. JAKE MILFORD—TRADED FOR TWO HOCKEY NETS   234

93. THE WRONG METZ WON THE MOST CUPS   235

94. TAKING A BATH WITH TUBBY   238

95. FIRED BECAUSE OF A HOT POKER HAND   239

96. THE NEAR-KIDNAPPING OF A RANGERS STAR   240

97. THERE WAS MAGIC IN LEONE'S BIG WINE BOTTLE   241

98. THE MOST UNUSUAL GOAL BY A GOALIE   245

99. HOW A LEAGUE PRESIDENT CREATED PHONY HOCKEY GAMES AND GOT AWAY WITH IT 247

100. THE NAKED GOALIE WAS GRATTOONY   249

101. WHEN THE ABSOLUTELY PERFECT GOAL NET WASN'T SO PERFECT AFTER ALL   250

Acknowledgements

Any book that lists 101 incredible feats in any sport—
let alone hockey—is a feat in itself and that explains
why the author has a bushel of "thanks" to go around.

For starters I'm indebted to several interns who did scrupulous and often tiresome research to extract such facts as Fern Gauthier's inability to "shoot the puck in the ocean," not to mention discovering which *really* was Uncle Sam's greatest hockey team—the (Baltimore) Coast Guard Cutters, circa 1942-1944.

Thus, in alphabetical order I do a deep bow of appreciation to my all-star cast of Allyson Gronowitz, Michael Rappaport, and Jordan Schoem who not only manned the barricades—that is, my office—during the lengthy NHL lockout of 2012-2013 but unearthed gem after nifty gem that guarantees that this will be a first-class read. Without their firm support, finishing the book would truly have been an incredible feat.

Others who pitched in with their expertise include Dan Friedman, Alec Kessler, Jared Lane, Michael Leboff, Bill Martin, and Brian McCormack and Dan Ronayne, who delivered a remarkably timely assist when it counted most.

Instead of 101 incredible feats there would be a grand total of none had it not been for the creativity of our worthy editors at Skyhorse, led by the indefatigable Julie Ganz.

Were it not for their idea, The Maven would have been left to ice the puck or, in this case, the book.

I deeply appreciate their involvement from beginning to publication.

Not to be overlooked is The Hockey Maven-ess in our house, my dear wife, Shirley, who—if truth be told—knows a lot more hockey than I do; except that she never saw either Fern Gauthier nor the Coast Guard Cutters play.

You get the point; I'm grateful, appreciative, and indebted to you all.

Foreword

Hockey is a slippery game—it's played on ice.
—Emile (The Cat) Francis,
former general manager, New York Rangers

The Cat—who did enjoy nine lives as an NHL goaltender
and executive—knew whereof he spoke.

Hockey on the NHL level remains the most artistic,
violent, and passionate of all the major sports.

And the most zany.

Think about it for a moment; the players are performing on
artificial feet (skates), on an artificial surface (ice) with artificial
arms (sticks), and a funny, little, hard, black biscuit called a puck,
hockey's version of a hand grenade.

In such circumstances, it shouldn't be a surprise that with
all the craziness that erupts over three, twenty-minute periods,
fights break out as well. Some of the bouts such as the *fifteen-
minute* classic between Johnny (Maroosh) Mariucci of the Chicago
Blackhawks and Black Jack Stewart of the Detroit Red Wings have
been more remarkable—and bloody—than goals scored.

Having watched hockey games on all levels of competition
since 1939—my first live game was at Madison Square Garden

when I was seven years old—I can safely say that I've witnessed some of the most incredible feats of all.

Some have been hilarious such as the episode when a slumping Detroit player named Fern Gauthier had to prove that he could shoot the puck into the ocean off a Manhattan pier by actually doing so.

Some feats are incredible in other ways.

For example, I was there the night that Chicago Blackhawks winger Bill (Wee Willie) Mosienko scored three goals in *twenty-one seconds.* Now there's an accomplishment that never, ever, will be duplicated. As a matter of fact, now that I think about it, I still can't believe that it actually happened. But it did, and Rangers goalie Lorne Anderson was an unfortunate witness—and victim.

Speaking of unusual exploits, I also watched from the Madison Square Garden press box the night an Andy Bathgate backhand shot caught unmasked Montreal goalie Jacques Plante smack in the face. Bleeding profusely, Plante was helped from the ice and stitched up by the team doctor. When Plante returned, he was wearing a face mask; a device unheard of in those days of the six-team league NHL.

Plante was the first to do so and eventually every goaltender donned a shield to protect his good looks; or what was left of them.

Some, such as Hall of Famer Glenn Hall of the Blackhawks, resisted. But Hall would freely admit that goaltending without a mask was "Sixty minutes of hell." Before retiring as a member of the St. Louis Blues, Hall finally relented and donned the covering. Safer it was, but it bothered Mister Goalie so much that he decided to call it a career.

As you can tell by now, I sure enjoy covering the hockey scene and among my many reasons for staying with the game is the likelihood of yet another unlikely development to take place on— or off—the ice.

In the meantime, I hope you enjoy my choice of 101 incredible hockey feats.

Stan Fischler, New York, January 2013

I
Hockey History

1 | TORONTO'S "DREADED" THREE-GOAL LEAD

It seems like a cushion that any team would love to have, but through the years a three-goal advantage occasionally has turned into a disaster for clubs up by a trio of red lights. To some press box wags, it has become known as the "dreaded" three-goal lead.

But never in Stanley Cup playoff history has a calamitous collapse occurred like the one that befell the Toronto Maple Leafs on the night of May 13, 2013, at Boston's TD Garden in Game 7 of the Eastern Conference Quarterfinal series—winner-take-all.

Coached by Randy Carlyle, the Leafs led Boston 4-1 and appeared on the way to winning its first Stanley Cup Playoff series since 2004. There were less than eleven minutes separating the host Bruins from a humiliating upset or, as Boston coach Claude Julien put it, they were "on the ropes."

Toronto goalie James Reimer—a star for the visitors—appeared to have the situation well in hand as the overhead clock ticked toward the 9:10 mark of the third period. Anticipating almost certain defeat for their beloved Beantowners, scores of fans left their seats, heading for the exits. Suddenly, a few stopped in their tracks when the Bruins mounted a concerted attack, which culminated with Nathan Horton scoring at 9:18 of the period. It was 4-2 for the Leafs, who then went into a defensive shell, hoping to run out the clock.

For more than nine minutes the tactic worked and finally—desperately—with less than two minutes remaining, Julien pulled his netminder Tuukka Rask in favor of a sixth skater. Boston won the faceoff, whereupon captain Zdeno Chara blasted a shot from the point that forced Reimer to make a save, but he was unable to control the rebound. Boston's clutch scorer Milan Lucic pounced on the rebound and caged it with 82 seconds left to play. Now it was only 4-3 for the faltering Leafs. "We were running out of gas," recalled Carlyle.

Keeping Rask on the bench, Julien gambled on leaving his net open. Sure enough, Boston won the faceoff, drilling the puck deep into the Toronto zone. The Bruins' David Krejci got there first and ladled a pass to Patrice Bergeron, who was camped in the high slot. The French-Canadian forward wasted no time sending the puck behind Reimer at 19:09 and the score now was tied at four sending the game into overtime.

In the first sudden-death period, the Leafs regrouped and for six minutes played Boston even, but the relentless Bruins eventually stormed the Toronto zone, where Tyler Seguin forced Reimer to make another save. Once again the beleaguered goalie failed to control the rebound while receiving no help from his hapless defense.

While the visitors scrambled for position, the alert Bergeron raced to the right circle from where he fired the puck past Reimer. The time was 6:05 of the extra session and Boston's victory not only stunned millions of Toronto fans but established an NHL record as well. It marked the first time in Stanley Cup history that a team overcame a three-goal deficit in the third period of a playoff game and then went on to win the contest.

Morose as he sat in the Toronto dressing room, all Reimer could say was that he had "an empty feeling and there's nothing I can do about it."

The "dreaded" three-goal lead will do that, but never before in the manner that if stung the Maple Leafs on that spring night in Boston.

2 | THE SECOND-LONGEST GAME

Before Modere "Mud" Bruneteau scored the winning goal, in 1936, in the longest playoff game in NHL history, another third-stringer did likewise. Ken Doraty was the hero of the longest game ever played up until that point.

It was in 1933 when the hero—like Bruneteau—was a virtual unknown. In some ways, the "Doraty Game" was even stranger than what was to become the all-time marathon, and here's why.

The first round of the Stanley Cup playoffs between the Toronto Maple Leafs and Boston Bruins was tied at two apiece. The fifth game of the best-of-five series would be decided on Monday, April 3, 1933, at Maple Leaf Gardens.

That is, everyone thought the game would be settled on Monday night. Who would have dreamed that the skaters would be churning up the ice well past midnight and into Tuesday, April 4?

Already it had been a grand series. Boston had won the opener, 2-1, in sudden-death at Beantown, but the Leafs roared back to tie the series at Boston Garden in another sudden-death affair. The score was 1-0. Now the series switched to Toronto, where the Bruins triumphed 2-1—in sudden-death.

Desperate for young legs, Toronto manager Conn Smythe dressed amateur stars Bill Thoms and Charlie Sands, and ordered more ice time for Kenny Doraty, a 135-pound mite. All three came through like veterans, and the Leafs won the fourth game, 5-3, to tie the series and set the stage for a climactic fifth game. Fans lined up in the middle of the preceding night in the hopes of obtaining tickets for the finale, and by game time Maple Leaf Gardens was jammed with 14,540 rooters.

Their series had already proven so tight—three out of four games had gone into overtime—that nobody expected anything less than a tight battle, and nobody was disappointed. Goaltenders Lorne Chabot of the Leafs and Tiny Thompson of the Bruins were impeccably sharp. Chabot allowed one goal—to Alex Smith—in the third period, but it had been erased on an offsides call. As the buzzer sounded, signaling the end of regulation time, the scoreboard proclaimed: "BOSTON 0, TORONTO 0."

Neither team scored in the first sudden-death period, and there were those who believed that the longer the game continued, the better the Bruins' chances because some of Toronto's top players were among the skating wounded. Ace Bailey was playing with his shoulder taped tightly to keep it in place. Defenseman Red Horner was holding his stick with his one good hand, and (Gentleman) Joe Primeau had been released from the hospital that afternoon and still had an extremely tender foot.

On and on the game flowed, through a second overtime and a third. "Morning papers appeared in the rink," said Maple Leafs publicist Ed Fitkin, "and were sold as fast as they were produced. Midnight came and went, and still the battle went on. Fans both in and out of the rink were apparently determined to see it through. The players on the ice were dog-tired and near exhaustion."

Among the stars, Boston featured Eddie Shore, who didn't leave the ice for the first 60 minutes of action and then only took brief respites during overtime. King Clancy was equally inspiring for Toronto. "There wasn't a weakling out there," said Fitkin. "The fans knew it, and they began talking about the inhumanity of letting the game go on.

"They were saying the tension and strain might affect the players for the rest of their lives. NHL officials must have been thinking along the same lines, for when the fourth overtime session got underway they were trying to figure out the best way to settle the issue."

Joe Primeau almost made that issue academic. Benched because of the gravity of his injury, Primeau was finally pressed into action in the fourth sudden-death period to relieve the overworked Andy Blair and Bill Thoms. Upon seeing the dapper center skate onto the ice, the fans rose as one and gave him a thunderous ovation. As if inspired by his following, Primeau promptly orchestrated an attack, with King Clancy skating parallel with him toward the Boston goal. At the Bruins' blue line, Primeau skimmed a pass to Clancy, who took a few strides and fired the puck behind Thompson. The red light flashed, and Maple Leaf Gardens was rocked to its foundation.

So high was the decibel count that few onlookers realized, at first, that the whistle had blown, signaling an offsides. The goal was immediately disallowed. That was Primeau's big chance—the fourth overtime ground on to the 20-minute mark without a score. It was still a 0-0 deadlock, and the respective managers, Conn Smythe and Art Ross of Boston, decided to huddle in the hopes of settling the draw. The arch rivals, who normally couldn't agree on the time of day, decided to flip a coin to determine the winner; that is, provided their respective players would go along with the plan. With that, Smythe trooped into the Leafs' dressing room and reported the results of the meeting.

The news was greeted with disdain by the Leafs. "Those so-and-sos aren't going to beat us by any toss of the coin," shouted Harold Cotton. Utterly fatigued as he was, Cotton convinced Smythe that there was no way he would allow the decision to be decided by a toss of the coin. National Hockey League President Frank Calder agreed. "The game," said Calder, "must be fought to a finish, no matter how long it takes."

So the fifth overtime began and, once again, the Leafs seemed to have victory in their grasp. The doughty Cotton snared a loose puck behind the Bruins' net, circled in front, and attempted to shift the rubber between Thompson's skate and the goal post. But the Boston defenders piled on Cotton, who believed he had jabbed the puck home. The referee whistled play to a halt, and Cotton argued that a Boston player had fished it out before the referee had seen the rubber. Cotton was overruled, and the fifth overtime period ended with the score 0-0 and the time well past 1:30 a.m.

Nobody talked about a toss-of-the-coin anymore. It would be a duel to the death, and when the sixth sudden-death period began, the respective teams played "kitty-bar-the-door" hockey in the extreme. "The scoring thrusts," said Fitkin, "sporadic as they were, lacked the sting of authority and were utterly incapable of drawing blood."

The Bruins still were attempting to exploit as much of the indomitable Eddie Shore as possible, but time was taking its toll on The Edmonton Express. As the overhead clock ticked past the four-minute mark, Shore had the puck in his own zone.

"He looked dead beat," said Fitkin, "and he was. Eddie needed a rest and was trying to make an offside pass to one of his mates and thus stop play. Shore finally spotted Joe Lamb in the clear and slid the puck toward him."

Eddie Shore—arguably the toughest defenseman of all time and the most intense taskmaster of club owners when Shore ran the Springfield Indians./
Associated Press

But the rubber never reached Lamb. Andy Blair, Toronto's lanky mustachioed center, detected Shore's plan and intercepted the pass. In one motion, Blair followed through with a pass to his right wing, Doraty, who took it in stride.

The fragile forward skated about three strides and then shot the puck past Thompson's pads and into the net. The light went on and, this time, there was no calling it back. Yet, for a moment, the fans were peculiarly silent. "The crowd," Fitkin recalled, "seemed unable to comprehend the fact. When they did, however, bedlam broke loose. People cheered, shouted, danced, threw programs, hats, anything they could get their hands on, while Doraty was being mobbed by his mates."

The time was 1:55 a.m. The puck went into the net at 4:46 of the sixth overtime period—after a total of 104 minutes and 46 seconds of overtime was played. Up until that point, it was the longest NHL game in history (a record that held for three years), and Doraty became an instant national hero. "Countless oldsters across the country," said *Toronto Star* columnist Milt Dunnell, "will recall how they finally fell into the sack, shortly before the dawn's early light, with the name of Ken Doraty still ringing in their ears."

Doraty's record was broken on March 24-25 at Montreal's Forum when Modere (Mud) Bruneteau scored for the Red Wings at 16:30 of the sixth overtime to give Detroit a 2-1 win over the Montreal Maroons. "But I was the first," Doraty insisted. "I bet more people remember my goal than the one that guy—what's his name—Bruneteau scored."

3 | HOW HOCKEY'S FIRST MAJOR STRIKE LED TO NEW YORK GETTING ITS FIRST NHL TEAM

The only major players' strike in National Hockey League history occurred in 1925. The result was dramatic. The players were suspended and fined, and the NHL left Hamilton for New York. What's more, the strike and resulting league action deprived the Tigers of a chance to play for the Stanley Cup.

One of those involved was Wilfred Thomas "Shorty" Green, the Tigers' captain. Although the Hall of Fame biography describes him as a spokesman for the strikers, that role was played by Redvers "Red" Green, a top scorer and one of three players who had scored five goals in one game in the 1924-25 season.

With the extension of the schedule, the playoff format was changed. The second- and third-place teams—Montreal Canadiens and Toronto St. Patricks—were to play off, and the winner would play the Tigers, who had finished first. The survivor would then face the Western Canada champions for the cup.

Red Green drew attention to the fact that he had signed a two-year contract the previous season, calling for a 24-game schedule. Noting he had already played more than 30 games and was being asked to play more, he and his teammates demanded an extra $200.

Frank Calder, the NHL president, refused to give in to the strikers and ruled that the semifinal winner would represent the league in the Cup final.

The Canadiens defeated Toronto, 3-2 and 2-0, and advanced against the Victoria Cougars. Led by Jack Walker and Frank Fredrickson, the Cougars won the best-of-five series three games to one and captured the Stanley Cup.

The Tigers were suspended in April and fined $200 each. Then the team was sold to a New York group headed by gambler Bill Dwyer for $75,000 and appeared in 1925-26 as the Americans. They opened in the new Madison Square Garden before a crowd of 17,000.

Among Tigers players who were reinstated and made the jump to the Americans, besides the two Greens, were Billy Bauch, the 1924-25 Hart Trophy winner and Most Valuable Player in the NHL, Ken Randall, Alec McKinnon, Charlie Langlois, Mickey Roach, Edmond Bouchard, and goalie Vernon "Jumping Jake" Forbes. In addition, the Americans obtained "Bullet Joe" Simpson from the Edmonton Eskimos and Earl Campbell from the Ottawa Senators.

The team finished fourth, beating out Toronto and the Canadiens. What's more, the schedule was again extended—to 36 games—but there was no more strike talk.

4 | THE NHL'S MOST INCREDIBLE FIGHT

The legendary comedian Rodney Dangerfield always got a laugh when he said, "I went to a boxing match and a hockey game broke out." The inference, of course, is that hockey and fighting are virtually synonymous. Over the years, some of the most notorious hockey fights have commanded more attention—then and now—than some of the best games.

Eddie Shore vs. Muzz Patrick or Lou Fontinato vs. Gordie Howe are among those bouts that are still discussed to this day. But they were small potatoes compared with *the* biggest hockey fight of all-time. It had to be the biggest because every single player—including the goalies—were involved.

Perhaps the most incredible aspect of the bloodletting was the fact that the player who inspired the riot never actually saw the battles unfold. It happened this way:

Kenny Reardon, the rambunctious Montreal Canadiens defenseman, had one thing in mind as he stickhandled across the Madison Square Garden ice on March 16, 1947—freeze the puck. "Dick Irvin, our coach, had bawled the hell outta me for losing the puck and the game last time we were in New York," said Reardon. "I wasn't going to let that happen again."

Montreal was leading the Rangers 4-3 with only 32 seconds left in the game. If the powerful visitors could hold the lead, they'd clinch first place and a new prize of $1,000 for each player the NHL was giving away that year. The downtrodden Rangers, on the other hand, needed the win to stave off elimination from a playoff berth.

As Reardon cruised over the blue line, his overwhelming desire to nurse the puck got the best of him and he committed an egregious hockey sin—he fixed his eyes on the black rubber disk and forgot to look where he was going. The next thing he knew, Bryan Hextall's body loomed menacingly in front of him. Reardon bounced off Hextall like a pinball, right into Cal Gardner's waiting stick, which obligingly bludgeoned Reardon across the mouth. "My upper lip," Ken said, "felt as if it had been sawed off my face!"

Reardon finally was revived by Dr. Vincent Nardiello and escorted to the Garden's medical room along a route that might as well have been a minefield. His chief obstacles included the Rangers' bench, three rows of hostile fans, and an alleyway heavily populated with anti-Montreal guerrillas. As Reardon passed the New York bench, Phil Watson suggested that his mangled lip was not nearly enough punishment for him, and as Reardon bolted for Watson, a policeman intervened.

Then came the backbreaker. Up popped a fan brandishing a fist. "Reardon!" he shouted, "I've been waiting a long time for you to get it, you louse!"

"That did it," said Kenny. "I swung my stick at him—then a cop grabbed me from behind and I fell." The disturbance aroused the Rangers, who rose from their seats out of natural curiosity. From a distant vantage point from the Canadiens' bench, it looked as if Reardon was about to get ganged up on, heavily outnumbered.

"Get the hell over there," implored coach Irvin, standing on his bench. And so the Flying Frenchmen poured over the boards like Marines onto Normandy. When the first platoon reached the front, they were somewhat dismayed to find that the Rangers had not laid a stick on Reardon. Instead of retreating peacefully, the Canadiens began brawling with the fans. A posse of special police tried to disperse the mob, but they would have had a better chance of teaming a herd of rhinos.

And so commenced what *The New York Times* dubbed, "the grandest mass riot in local NHL history." Montreal captain Butch Bouchard, who led the stampede, clouted a bald-headed specta-tor with his stick, while goalie Bill Durnan and Maurice Richard sought other prospective victims. The sight of their defense-less followers being manhandled by the stick-swinging enemy disturbed the Rangers, so somebody on the Blueshirts yelled "Charge!" and the counterattack was underway.

Within seconds, the Rangers wiped out Montreal's beach-head, forcing the invaders to regroup at center ice, where four main events were already in progress: (1) Maurice Richard vs. Bill Juzda; (2) Bill Moe vs. Bill Durnan; (3) Hal Laycoe vs. Leo Lamoureux; and (4) Butch Bouchard vs. Bryan Hextall. The Marquis of Queensbury would have sanctioned the Moe-Durnan and Laycoe-Lamoureux bouts, but the others were strictly back-alley affairs.

Moe, who had been ordered not to play because of a shoulder injury, floored the heavily padded Durnan with a roundhouse right to the face. Laycoe and Lamoureux flailed away at each other in a fierce toe-to-toe encounter that only ended because the two were too tired to throw any more punches. Meanwhile, "Rocket" Richard broke his stick over Juzda's head, snapping the shaft in two. Juzda arose slowly, like a Frankenstein monster, and tackled Richard, bringing him down violently.

In another incident, Bouchard ripped Hextall's stick away from him and flattened him with a huge punch. Having dispensed with Durnan, Moe cracked a stick over Bouchard's head, and Butch didn't even seem to notice that he had been hit. One of the more bizarre preliminary bouts involved Murph Chamberlain of Montreal and Joe Cooper of the Rangers. When Murph missed a wild uppercut, Cooper replied with a sizzling right that catapulted Chamberlain clear over the sideboards and deposited him in a front row seat.

Juzda then excused himself from Richard, picked up a stray stick and poled Buddy O'Connor, breaking his jaw. "It became an almost endless fight," wrote Bill Wittig of the *New York Sun*. "No sooner was one group of players quieted down than another would start at it again. In one span, there were fifteen fights going on between players, and not even eight Garden policemen could restore order."

At this point, organist Gladys Gooding lit into "The Star Spangled Banner," but judging by the reaction she might well have been playing "Broadway Boogaloo." Peacemakers were as contemptuously regarded as the enemy. When Frank Boucher offered to mediate the Ken Mosdell-Edgar Laprade dispute, Mosdell murderously swung his stick at Boucher, causing the Rangers manager to seek asylum behind the dasher board.

The only players to escape unblemished were the normally violent Phil Watson of the Rangers and George Allen of Montreal. Watson said it wasn't a mere accident: "I grabbed hold of Allen," Watson explained, "and said, 'Look, George, what's the sense of getting all tangled up? Whaddya say we stand on the side and watch this one?' He said play, so we did. It was the best fight we had ever saw."

The fight lasted 20 minutes, the armistice finally induced by mass exhaustion. When it came time to report the offenders, referee Hayes obviously suffered a fit of compassion—he handed out only three penalties, 10-minute misconducts to Richard, Juzda, and Chamberlain. The last half-minute was not without incident either. Tony Leswick of the Rangers attempted to impale Durnan, while the usually pacific Ab DeMarco erupted against Mosdell.

As the final buzzer sounded, police averted another great way by immediately herding the players into their respective dressing rooms. Montreal had won the game 4-3 and, but for one man, the Canadiens toasted their victory (and escape from Manhattan) on the train all the way home.

That one disconsolate man was Kenny Reardon, who needed fourteen stitches to close his banged-up lip. But it wasn't the injury that bothered Reardon so much.

"I was the guy who started the whole damn fight," Reardon remembered, "but, believe it or not, I never saw it. Right after the cop knocked me down, I got up and walked to the clinic. I didn't find out about the fight until the game was over and the guys came back into the bloody room all cut. Sorta burns me up. I coulda had a great time!"

5 | THE BOOTLEGGER AND THE BODYCHECKERS

Fans of the popular HBO television series *Boardwalk Empire* know all about bootlegging during the Prohibition Era. One of the stars of the show—the actor who plays Lucky Luciano, Vincent Piazza—once was a hockey player himself at Villanova University.

But, actually, there was a genuine bootlegging hockey story that involved the NHL. As it happened, when Madison Square Garden (III) opened in 1925, the first NHL team there was called the New York Americans. They had as much color as their Star Spangled uniforms and their owner, millionaire bootlegger "Big Bill" Dwyer, put together. That's a lot of color.

Dwyer was a story in himself; brought up within rock-throwing distance of the old Madison Square Garden, he became a prominent peddler of illegal alcohol during the zany Prohibition days of the twenties. The fact that Big Bill served a couple of years in Sing Sing prison didn't seem to matter. Everybody—cops, cronies, customers—thought he was an unusual chap.

The fact is, he was. Big Bill never heard of ice hockey when sportswriter Bill McBeth told him he ought to buy a team and play it out of New York. But Dwyer wrote a check for $75,000 and bought the entire Hamilton, Ontario, Tigers franchise.

Today, $75,000 would be the going rate for a standard minor-league defenseman.

The year was 1925, and for the following decade it was better than even money that wherever the Americans were, on or off the ice, all hell would be breaking loose. Tall Thomas Patrick "Tommy" Gorman was the first manager of the Amerks, as they were nicknamed, and a more ideal personality could not have been found for the job. He knew his hockey and he loved a good gag, and there was a surplus of both with the Americans.

As for the hockey, it was abundantly competent, if not sensational. The team consisted of the Green brothers, Shorty and Red, who flanked center Billy Burch, giving the Amerks a line of extraordinary ability; forward "Bullet" Joe Simpson, who had a shot as exciting as Bobby Orr's; and defensemen "Big Leo" Reise (whose son was later to play for the Rangers); Alec Kinnon; and Lionel "Big Train" Conacher, voted Canada's Athlete of the Half Century. As for goalie, the Amerks had Roy "Shrimp" Worters, who emerged as one of the better small goaltenders of all time.

In those days money was a piddling matter to the Americans. Even though Dwyer was taking a modest loss on his hockey team, he was raking in so much on his bootlegging business that he couldn't spend it fast enough. What's more, hockey was catching on in New York, and the instant success of the Americans inspired Madison Square Garden to go out and form a second New York team, the Rangers.

The Amerks forced tough Newsy Lalonde to quit as coach after the 1926-27 season, when the club did not reach the playoffs in its division. Shorty Green took over as bench manager the next year and lasted exactly one season. They finished second in their division, the best they'd ever do, but were eliminated in the first round of the playoffs by the Ranger counterparts.

Nevertheless, manager Tommy Gorman decided to take the club on a postseason exhibition trip that eventually brought them to Portland, Oregon, for a game with the local team. By this time, all the players knew that Dwyer, a first-class bootlegger, also had a first-class mob, and it was not unusual for some of his all-star gangsters to show up at hockey games.

Unknown to the Amerks, the Portland management had a unique way of announcing that a period of play had ended. At the end of the first period, a loud gunshot blast went off and the Amerks reacted appropriately. Gorman remembered it well:

"Johnny Sheppard and Tex White fell right off the bench, while Roy Worters and Lionel Conacher raced like dogs from the vicinity of our net to the nearest boards and scrambled over the boards. A couple of our guys on the ice were so startled, that they lost their balance and fell flat on their behinds."

Maybe the last face was symbolic. The Americans finished fifth the next season, and eventually Dwyer was arrested and convicted of bootlegging. While Dwyer was in the penitentiary, the club's debts began mounting. By the time he got out in 1935, the bills were enormous and Dwyer was broke. The team needed a multi-millionaire to bail them out. Fortunately, the father of the American's superb defenseman Mervyn "Red" Dutton, just happened to be a multi-millionaire.

The senior Mr. Dutton's contracting business in western Canada was doing so well that Red could have played hockey for nothing if he wanted to. The wealthy Duttons provided the money to keep the team going and continued to do so even after the illustrious Dwyer passed out of the picture the very next season.

6 | THE NIGHT THE RANGERS GOT TALKED OUT OF A PLAYOFF BERTH

Many weird events have taken place during the National Hockey League's history, but nothing could be stranger than a team being talked out of qualifying for a playoff berth.

But it did happen, and the victim was the New York Rangers and especially its power play specialist Max Bentley. Here's how it all happened:

During the 1953-54 season, Rangers manager Frank Boucher signed future Hall of Famer Max Bentley to a one-year contract. Although Max's three Stanley Cup years with the Toronto Maple Leafs were well behind him, "The Dipsy-Doodle Dandy from Delisle" still had some good moves in him.

Boucher used Bentley as a point man on the Blueshirts power play along with Camille "The Eel" Henry, who would win the Calder Trophy as the NHL's best freshman.

Throughout the first half of the season, New York was in a neck and neck race with Boston for the fourth and final playoff berth. After the 1954 New Year, the Rangers boss pulled an ace out of his sleeve.

He persuaded Max's older brother Doug—also a future Hall of Famer—out of retirement. At the time, Doug had been player-coach of the Rangers farm team in Saskatoon. Although Doug had been reluctant to make an NHL comeback after being out of the league for several years, the thought of being reunited with Max was the convincing argument.

After all, the two had starred for years on the Chicago Blackhawks "Pony Line" along with Bill "Wee Willie" Mosienko before Max was traded to Toronto in November 1947. Having been apart six years, the brothers were tickled with the reunion and responded immediately with a big win over the Bruins in New York.

The performance convinced Doug that he should finish the season with New York in the hopes of helping the Rangers get past Boston into a playoff berth. However, the question troubling Boucher was whether Max and Doug could maintain their brisk pace to the end.

"The opposition started to pound us," said Doug. "The Bruins sent big fellows like Eddie Sandford and Cal Gardner after us. They hit us, leaned on us, and fouled us whenever possible."

When the Rangers played Detroit at Madison Square Garden, Glen Skov of the Red Wings actually speared the "R" off the front of Max's jersey and provoked the younger Bentley into one of his rare fights. The most subtle strategy, and ultimately the most effective, was employed by Bruins coach, Lynn Patrick, when Boston played the Rangers late in the season.

Aware that Max was a hypochondriac, Lynn instructed his players to comment casually on how terrible he looked. It was to be done nonchalantly, but regularly. "Cal Gardner did it best," Lynn recalled. "After a while, Max seemed to get depressed and more depressed, and the quality of his play began slipping."

Nevertheless, it was touch-and-go between the Rangers and the Bruins until their last meeting in Boston Garden. The feeling was that if Muzz Patrick could get his team to beat older brother Lynn's Bruins on that night, the Rangers would make it.

Max and Doug were still making beautiful music with Edgar Laprade as long as Max was healthy and the club had developed an *espirit de corps*.

But they hadn't found a way to cure Max's hypochondria, and that's how the Rangers became the only club in the NHL annals to be talked out of a playoff berth. The culprit was Gardner, an ex-Ranger and former Maple Leaf.

Gardner: "I had been Max's teammate on the Maple Leafs when we won the Cups in 1949 and 1951, and we had been room-mates. Nobody knew Max better than I did, but now we weren't teammates anymore and this was a game we had to win. As soon as we got on the ice for warm-ups, I made a beeline for Max and told him straight out he seemed sick to me and that he should see a doctor. Whenever we'd pass, I'd bring it up again. By game time, Max was a wreck and couldn't do a thing for New York that night. Naturally, we beat the Rangers."

The standings show that the Blueshirts finished six games behind Boston, but had they won that game in Beantown, the standings might have very well been reversed.

7 | HOCKEY'S AMAZING BROTHER ACTS

O f all the major sports, none can compare with hockey when it comes to brothers playing on the same team. No less than ten brother acts have been featured in the NHL and many of them—such as Maurice and Henri Richard—include Hall of Famers.

The following—in chronological order—are hockey's same-team brother acts:

1. **SPRAGUE AND ODIE CLEGHORN**: These Cleghorns were gems with the Montreal Canadiens from 1921-22 through 1924-25. Odie was more offensive-minded then his brother, while Sprague was a rough, tough defenseman. Both Cleghorns are in the Hall of Fame and were the closest of siblings. Only a few hours before Sprague's funeral was set to commence in 1956, Odie was found dead of a heart attack.

2. **BILL AND BUN COOK:** The Cooks, both Hall of Famers, had no shortage of dual accomplishments. They played ten years together for the New York Rangers, winning the Stanley Cup twice in 1927-28 and 1932-33. They were both All-Stars in the 1930-31 season, with Bill on the first team and Bun on the second. In the 1932-33 season, Bill finished first in points for a Rangers player, with Bun coming in second.

3. **DOUG AND MAX BENTLEY:** These Bentleys benefited greatly from playing with one another while on the Chicago Blackhawks. Although they never won a Cup together, they were among the top ten scorers of the NHL three separate seasons, including in 1942-43 when Doug won the Art Ross Trophy with 73 points and Max finished only three points behind him with 70. In 1954, the two brothers, who were in their thirties, were reunited. In their reunion debut in January 1954 for the New York Rangers, they each had four points while beating the Boston Bruins 8-3. They are both members of the NHL Hall of Fame.

4. **MAURICE AND HENRI RICHARD:** Incredibly, the brothers won the Stanley Cup together for five consecutive seasons between 1956-1960 with the Montreal Canadiens. "The Rocket" and "The Pocket Rocket" combined for 238 goals and 538 points in that span. Both brothers went on to Hall of Fame careers, winning more Cups and awards over the course of their extraordinary careers.

5. **BOBBY AND DENNIS HULL:** Both the "Golden Jet" and Dennis were known as scoring machines during their stint with the Chicago BlackHawks from 1964-1971. They amassed 550 goals and 1,032 points in that span, including a combined 88 goals and 171 points in the 1968-69 season.

6. **FRANK AND PETER MAHOVLICH:** The "Big M" (Frank) and Peter played together on two separate teams, bringing a "winning" mentality with them. They played for the Detroit Red Wings for two seasons before leaving for Montreal, where they won the Stanley Cup twice in 1971 and 1973.

7. **BRENT AND DUANE SUTTER:** Of all the brother acts, this family is quite significant in hockey history. With six separate brothers all playing in the NHL at one point or another, it was only a matter of time before two of them made magic while

playing together. Brent and Duane won Stanley Cups in 1982 and 1983 with the New York Islanders.

8. **PETER, MARIAN, AND ANTON STATSNY:** This unheralded Slovakian trio played together for the Quebec Nordiques for four successful seasons from 1981-85. They were offensive dynamos and together scored 390 goals and 1,029 points. Their most fruitful season was the first year they played together for Quebec, combining for 300 points in 1981-82.

9. **HENRIK AND DANIEL SEDIN:** Amazingly, there are two sets of twins who played in the NHL hailing from Sweden. The Sedins and Henrik and Joel Lundqvist. However, it is Henrik and Daniel, who play together for the Vancouver Canucks, who get all the accolades. In 2010, Henrik won the Hart Trophy as the NHL's Most Valuable Player, with Daniel following up as a finalist for the award the next season. Each brother won the NHL scoring crown, which is the first and only brotherly tandem to do so.

10. **ERIC AND JORDAN STAAL:** It was always the dream of the three Staal brothers—Marc, Eric, and Jordan—to play on the same team. For most of their NHL careers, Eric was on Carolina, Marc on New York, and Jordan on Pittsburgh. But, in the summer of 2012, the Hurricanes obtained Jordan in a trade for Brandon Sutter, Brian Dumoulin, and a draft choice. As for their accomplishments, Eric won the Stanley Cup in 2005-06 and has three All-Star Game appearances. Jordan was on the NHL's All-Rookie Team in 2007, won the Stanley Cup in 2009 with the Pittsburgh Penguins, and was a finalist for the Frank J. Selke award in 2010, which honors the forward with the most skill in the defensive aspect of the game. Meanwhile, Marc emerged as one of the Rangers' defensive stalwarts, arguably the best of the Blueshirts' backliners.

8 | THE OTHER OLYMPIC MIRACLE, IN 1960

When discussing Uncle Sam's Olympic heroics in hockey, most of the so-called experts zero-in on the 1980 Gold Medal triumph at Lake Placid, New York.

Unfortunately, most of the sages overlook an even bigger victory two decades earlier—thanks to an unknown goaltender named Jack McCartan. In 1960, the hockey world stood in awe of Jack McCartan and the U.S. Olympic Team. Players such as Ken Yackel, Bill Christian, John Mayasich, and Tommy Williams became household names overnight, not to mention McCartan and the U.S. coach Jack Riley.

"We were definitely underdogs," said Riley. "We couldn't possibly win a gold medal. At least that's what they all said before we hit the ice." Yet, the U.S. Olympians, with McCartan in goal, would do more to bolster the prestige of American hockey than any other team since the 1938 Chicago Blackhawks, a club that was sprinkled with Americans, had won the Stanley Cup.

Their most formidable opponents would be the Soviets and the Canadians. It was not believed to be even remotely possible that the Americans could topple either of these power teams. McCartan's first challenge was against the Swedish National Team, traditionally a strong-skating, hard-shooting club. The favored Swedes were routed, 6-3.

Murmurs about the American squad began filtering around Olympic Village. The murmuring got louder after the U.S. skaters demolished Germany, 9-1. Again, McCartan virtually built a wall in front of his 4x6 net. Now, the Americans were scheduled to meet Canada's National Team for the first time. Almost incredibly, the Americans defeated the Canadians, 2-1, and then knocked off the Soviet sextet, 3-2, then Czechoslovakia, Swedes again, and finally West Germany.

Suddenly, the Americans found themselves in the unlikely position of being in sight of a gold medal. They had three games—three obstacles—ahead of them: Canada, Russia, and Czechoslovakia. The Canadians looked like the better team as they poured volley after volley at goalie McCartan. "All I could see were streaks of green Canadian jerseys," said McCartan.

McCartan made 39 saves, most of them difficult, and allowed only one goal. "He made one incredible save after another," said Riley. The Americans scored twice and won the match, 2-1. On Saturday, February 27, the Americans faced off against the Soviet team. More than ten thousand spectators jammed Blyth Arena for the contest while millions watched the game on television. "It was," said McCartan in a moment of understatement, "a very exciting time of my life."

After two periods, the Soviets had beaten McCartan twice, but so had the Americans, who scored two goals. More importantly, the Americans proved that they could skate with the fleet Russians. For nearly 15 minutes of the final period, the rivals tested goalies McCartan and Nikolai Puchkov, and neither gave an inch—until 14:59 of the period.

The Americans won the game, 3-2, and only one more opponent blocked the Americans' bid for a gold medal—Czechoslovakia.

Against the Czechs, McCartan was less than flawless. He allowed four goals after two periods, while the Americans had scored three. At that point, a strange twist of fate helped the Americans.

Nikholai Sologubov, crack defensemen for the Russian National Team, visited the Americans' dressing room and offered Riley some advice. "He suggested that our players take some oxygen to restore their prep," Riley recalled. "As it turned out, some of our guys took his advice."

The Americans stormed out onto the ice and nearly knocked the Czechs out of their skates. Roger Christian alone accounted for three goals in the last period. He tied the score at 4-4 at 5:50 of the period. Then Bill Cleary put the Americans ahead, 5-4, and followed that with a power-play goal. Within a 30-second span, Roger Christian and Billy Cleary scored, and then Roger closed the scoring at 17:56 for the sixth and final goal of the period for Uncle Sam's skaters. Meanwhile, McCartan fervently held the fort, and America won the game, 9-4, and its first Olympic gold medal in hockey. "For us," said McCartan, "it was a special feeling because something like that never happened before that time."

It is doubtful whether St. Paul-born John William "Jack" McCartan would have made it as a big-league goaltender had he not been a part of the Cinderella United States hockey team that upset Canada, Czechoslovakia, and the Soviet Union to win a Gold Medal at Squaw Valley in 1960. McCartan historians coincided with a decline in the fortunes of the New York Rangers during the 1959-60 season.

General manager Muzz Patrick was looking for someone to hype the gate late in the campaign, and McCartan was a natural. Amid suitable tub-thumping, the Rangers brought McCartan to Broadway, replacing the veteran goalie Al Rollins, who incidentally was playing superb goal for New York.

Those who thought McCartan wouldn't last long among NHL stars such as Gordie Howe and Jen Beliveau were wrong. McCartan beat the mighty Detroit Red Wings his first game, even stopping Howe on a breakaway! Was it a fluke? Absolutely not.

McCartan played three more games through the conclusion of the 1959-60 season, and when the ice had cleared he had allowed a grand total of only seven goals in four games, good for a stingy 1.75 goals against average. All signs pointed to a bright and beautiful big-league career for McCartan and, naturally, he was invited back to the Rangers for the 1960-61 campaign. But within eight games it was clear that Jack's bubble had burst, and he was a shade of the performer who had wowed 'em in Squaw Valley and then, briefly, at Madison Square Garden.

"The reason why I was able to get a chance with the Rangers," said McCartan, "was because of all the publicity. The ratio between the publicity and my possibilities of actually making it to the NHL was about 80% publicity and 20% fact. But the Rangers made me the offer—the thrill of my life—and naturally I accepted. All in all, I would say that I had some fair success and at other times it was very hard.

"The NHL was a good league at the time. I was up against players like Bobby Hull, Gordie Howe, Alex Delvecchio, and all the great Montreal players. It didn't last all that long, but I wouldn't have changed a thing. I was happy enough just to get to the NHL, to compete, to see what it was like. I always loved the game of hockey, love it today and always will."

McCartan is best remembered for stopping Howe and the Red Wings and stopping a thunderous punch from then rookie Reggie Fleming of the Chicago Blackhawks during a tough match at Madison Square Garden. "It started with a fight between Fleming and Eddie Shore of our club. Shack was cooling off after they broke it up and he skated to center ice. Fleming picked up a stick and started up to center ice after Shack. Well, I didn't know about the guy and thought he was going to hatchet Shack with his stick. So, I slid my own stick up toward center ice so Shack could pick it up and defend himself.

"Well, nothing happened up there, so I skated up to get my stick back. So happened that Fleming was skating back to pick up his gloves behind the net. As we passed, he suckered me with a punch to the head. That was it, and I had all I could do to stay on my feet. He hit me with a good shot and I saw stars," remembered McCartan.

Grateful for the opportunity to play for the Rangers, McCartan took his demotion to the minors like the trooper that he was.

9 | A BROTHERLY BROADCASTING TRIFECTA

During the 1982-83 National Hockey League season, three brothers were simultaneously broadcasting the play-by-play action of NHL games. Marv Albert, the elder statesman of the trio, broadcasted home games for the New York Rangers on WNEW-Radio in New York City. Albert had been broadcasting the Rangers since 1967, and at the time, was in his fifteenth year calling games. Marv's kid brother, Steve, was play-by-play commentator for SportsChannel, the cable television network that in 1982-83 handled home games for the New Jersey Devils. Al Albert, the middle man of the triumvirate, was behind the microphone for NHL games handled by the USA Network.

10 | HOW UNCLE SAM BEAT JOHNNY CANUCK TO PRO HOCKEY

The first professional hockey league was located in the United States, not Canada. Houghton, Michigan, was the focal point of the International Pro Hockey League, which was founded in 1904. It included representatives of Sault Sainte Marie, Michigan; St. Paul, Minnesota; St. Louis, Missouri; and Pittsburgh, Pennsylvania, each of which played exhibition games against the Portage Lakes team from Houghton. Sault Sainte Marie, Ontario, was the original Canadian entry in the league, which disbanded in 1907. Doctor J. L. Gibson, a defenseman from the Portage Lakes, was the founder of the IPHL.

11 | THE "PERFECT" GOALIE IS A HOAX

I t has been said that the perfect goaltender would be one whose measurements allowed him to cover all—or most of—the six feet wide by four feet high net. A Boston writer once claimed that he had found such an ideal netminder.

During the late 1950s, when the Boston Bruins were suffering through an endless drought, a Hub sportswriter named Roger Barry got a brainstorm. Barry, who covered hockey for the Quincy *Patriot-Ledger*, was so moved by the Bruins' plight that he wrote an article about the "discovery" of the utopian Bruins goalie. The man had a French name—on the order of Pierre Lafond—and he reportedly was discovered in the wilds of Northern Quebec.

What made lucky Pierre so ideal for the goalkeeping position, according to Barry, were his dimensions; he measured an ideal five-by-five—five feet tall and five feet wide—thereby enabling him to block all but a few inches of the goal area merely by standing still. In order to put the puck past him, the enemy would require either a crane or a blowtorch.

Publication of the "Perfect Pierre" story in the Boston Garden hockey program caused a wave of excitement around the National Hockey League, for this was truly an extraordinary find. Bruins fans were delirious with joy over the prospect of trimming the club's atrocious goals against average and opponents wondered just how they would cope with the Chinese Wall of a goalie.

The normally whimsical Barry was somewhat startled by the reaction to his story. "It was only a gag," he revealed to many who, somehow, had taken him seriously. "Mister Five-by-Five was merely a product of my imagination, not the Bruins' farm system."

But the beleaguered Boston hockey fans, who were prepared to cling to any thread of hope about their team, accepted the myth of Pierre Lafond and, at least temporarily, converted it into their own form of reality.

12 | HOW TO BECOME A TRAINER BY WALKING DOWN THE STREET

Nick Garen, who was a trainer in the National Hockey League, got his first job in 1946 while strolling around downtown Chicago after being discharged from the United States Air Corps. As he was window-shopping in the downtown Loop area, Garen—at the time his full name was Gurenovich—noticed a face he had seen somewhere in athletic circles. He thought for a moment and then decided to ask the gentleman in question: "Say, aren't you Ed Froélich?" Garen inquired, running up to the other.

"That's right," the other said. The man opposite Garen just happened to be the trainer for both the New York Yankees baseball team and the Chicago Blackhawks of hockey fame. "What can I do for you?" Froelich asked.

"Well," Garen explained, "I'm Nick Gurenovich. I know you've never heard of me, but I've heard a lot about you, and it's all been good. I know you're one of the best in the business. I used to see you at Yankee Stadium. I've sort of done some training myself with the armed service teams. It's kind of the job I'd like to work at permanently someday, but I know you have to be good to stick in your kind of business."

Nick explained that in the Air Force he worked with service teams at Kessler Field, Mississippi, and Chanute Field, Illinois. "Tell you what, Gurenovich," Froelich replied, "when you get home, drop me a line on your qualifications as a trainer. I might be able to do something for you."

All Froelich did was hire Garen as an assistant trainer for the Blackhawks during the 1946-47 season, and Nick remained in the NHL for the next four decades.

13 | WHY JOINING A UNION ONCE WAS DANGEROUS FOR HOCKEY PLAYERS

From the National Hockey League's inception in 1917, and for a half-century thereafter, there never was a union. During the late 1950s, a group of NHL stars tried to form a Player's Association. But they only succeeded in one area: they got the six team owners so angry that severe retribution was in order.

For example, Ted Lindsay, a Hall of Famer, who had been a lifelong member of the Detroit Red Wings, was dealt to the lowly Chicago Blackhawks; ditto for Toronto Maple Leaf's defensemen Jim Thomson and Gus Mortson.

New York Rangers Hall of Famer Andy Bathgate also felt the sting of management's ire.

"The fact that I was partly responsible for getting the Ranger players to join the association didn't endear me to management," Bathgate recalled, "and I began to hear rumblings that I would be traded. The animosity of the front office didn't surprise me. I knew that Doug Harvey, who had been a star with the Canadiens, was traded from Montreal.

"It was a strange situation at the time because the Rangers were considering all kinds of trades. They had the young center, Jean Ratelle, who had a great future and I had heard they were planning to trade him, too. I said at the time that they shouldn't trade Ratelle because he had a great future. Next thing I knew, he was traded."

14 | HOW A DETROIT FAN TURNED A LIVE OCTOPUS INTO A WINNING TEAM'S SYMBOL

Pete Cusimano never scored a goal in professional hockey. He never made a save, got an assist, or even served a two-minute bench penalty. Yet, Pete Cusimano is one of the most colorful and infamous characters hockey has ever known—Pete Cusimano threw octopi!

Pete and his brother Jerry were diehard Detroit Red Wing fans. During the 1952 playoffs the Wings were hot—they had already won seven consecutive contests and the two brothers felt that some symbolic sacrifice was in order.

"My dad was in the fish and poultry business," Pete explained. "Before the eight game in '52, my brother suggested, 'Why don't we throw and octopus on the ice for good luck? It's got eight legs and that might be a good omen for eight straight wins.'" It was a stroke of pure genius.

April 15, 1952, marked the first time Pete Cusimano heaved a half-boiled denizen of the deep over the protective glass and onto the ice of the Detroit Olympia. With one loud *splaaat!* the fate of the Wings' opponents was sealed. Yes hockey fans, Detroit won the Cup in 1952 and Cusimano, knowing a good thing when he saw one, continued to sling the slimy creatures in every Detroit playoff series for the next fifteen years.

"You ever smelt a half-boiled octopus?" asked Pete. "It ain't exactly Chanel No. 5 y'know." And with a maniacal gleam in his eye, he added, "You should see how the refs jumped."

15 | BABE RUTH, BUCK AND FRANK BOUCHER

Baseball and hockey are seldom thought of in the same breath, but there are occasions when they do happen to meet in strange circumstances.

One such circumstance came in the fall of 1930, just days before Rangers' center Frank Boucher reported to training camp. Boucher was working on his farm in Ottawa, when a friend phoned him that the fabled baseball stars Babe Ruth and Lou Gehrig of the New York Yankees were in town for an exhibition game, and that Frank and his brother George "Buck" were invited to play.

With the small park in Hull overflowing, and the fans eagerly waiting for Ruth to blast one out every time he came up at bat, there was tension between the team on which the Yankees stars played and the other squad, a group of amateurs, including Buck and Frank Boucher.

George was playing center field, a position he had never played in his life, and he was also using Frank's glove. Ruth was having a slightly off day, even though the opposing pitcher was grooving him on every delivery. The Sultan of Swat came up for the last time in the ninth.

Ruth knocked a deep dive to right center, and Buck Boucher tore after it. "Buck was playing way back in deepest center and toward right," relates Frank, "and as the ball started to come down it appeared that Buck might have a shot at it. Still, he was no outfielder. While the ball was descending, Buck ran several loose little circles under it and, finally, having misjudged it the whole way, stabbed across his body with my glove. He caught the ball in the webbing with one hand.

"By then Ruth was on his way to second and he just stopped and laughed and thumbed his nose to Buck, who was staring at the ball in amazement."

16 | THE OTHER STANLEY CUP

Rick Benej of Greenwich, New York, has been designing and selling the ultimate in table hockey games for years. Benej builds 100-150 of his exclusive ($575 each) models at his Adirondack workshop. And has made a thirty-year career of doing so. But table hockey—and the tournaments that go with it—did not originate in upstate New York.

Actually, the saga began with the author (Stan Fischler) and wife Shirley in 1968. We had a party in our West Side apartment, and half of the guests were what could best be described as eggheads, while the other half comprised of hockey fanatics.

We put the eggheads in the living room with classical music and the hockey nuts in the den with a table hockey set. Within minutes, the intellectual half of the party was facing-off against the puck pundits.

Competition was surprisingly intense; so much so that as a gag, Shirley donated one of her gravy bowls and named it the T. J. Rugg Trophy after a Detroit friend who promotes Monopoly tourneys.

Except the players didn't think it was a gag. The winners, Chris and Jon Cerf, sons of the late publisher Bennett Cerf, were challenged and another tourney was arranged the following year.

Soon word filtered down the grapevine, and out-of-town players demanded entry to the tourney.

Our apartment bulged to capacity for the 1969 event, covered by a national Canadian magazine and a major Toronto newspaper. The Cerfs won again, but my apartment lost; like $500 worth of damage was done—inadvertently, of course—by errant cigarette butts, spilled wine, and well-stepped-upon cheese. "Out!" demanded Shirley.

Eventually, the tournament was moved to the George Washington Hotel in Gramercy Park, but it was growing too fast for a small hotel; and too fast for the family to handle. Publisher Bob Stampleman, a former table hockey ace, retired to become WTHA chancellor, while I hung on as commissioner. Formal rules were established, along with affiliated leagues in Chicago, Detroit, and Toronto.

Celebrities such as author Randy Vataha and TV critic Marvin Kitman have been among the players. The gender barrier was broken in 1969, when Shirley played her first official match.

"The tourney grew so fast," said chancellor Stampleman, "that one night I arrived early for a Rangers game at Madison Square Garden, looked at the rink, and wondered where the rods were at the end of the arena!"

17 | THE RICHARD RIOT

No single event in hockey history caused as much commotion as the Maurice "Rocket" Richard riot that took place on March 13, 1955, at Boston Garden. Maurice Richard, *"L'enfant terrible"* of the Montreal Canadiens, was enjoying the most successful season of his lengthy career.

The most prolific goal-scorer in hockey, the Rocket appeared to be on his way to his first scoring championship. Boston led 4-2 with six minutes remaining in the third period. In an attempt to get the game tied up, Montreal coach Dick Irvin pulled his goalie right after Boston received a penalty, leaving Montreal up six players to Boston's four.

Richard glided over the Boston blue line when, without warning, Hal Laycoe's stick opened a gash on the side of Richard's head. Referee Frank Udvari signaled a delayed penalty to the Bruin because Montreal retained possession of the puck. By the time the whistle blew, Richard had returned to the blue line and noticed the blood spurting from his head.

The Rocket orbited. He skated over and smashed his stick over Laycoe's head and shoulders. Somehow, Laycoe stayed on his skates and dropped his gloves to fight it out. At the moment, Cliff Thompson, a linseman and former Bruins defenseman, rushed

Richard and yanked the stick away from him. But Richard was like a crazed bull; he grabbed another stick and slashed Laycoe until the wood cracked. Thompson clutched Richard, but the Rocket broke away and clubbed Laycoe again, until Thompson pulled Richard to the ice.

Richard was finally tossed out of the game and within hours, fans and NHL officials everywhere were demanding that NHL president Clarence Campbell severely punish the Rocket. On March 16, three days after the infamous bout, Campbell announced his decision: "Maurice Richard is suspended from playing in the remaining league and playoff games."

If Campbell had remained out of town he might have been safe, but he attended a game on March 17 at the Montreal Forum between Montreal and Detroit. By game time, the arena was surrounded by six hundred seething demonstrators, many carrying signs saying things such as, *"Vive Richard"* and *"A Bas Campbell"* (Down With Campbell). When the forum loudspeaker announced all seats were sold, a picketer yelled, "We don't want seats—we want Campbell!"

The demonstrators finally got their wish. When Campbell arrived at his seat with his secretary and her sister, fans noticed him immediately. The cascade of hoots were followed by volley upon volley of vegetables, eggs, bottles, and programs. "Go home, please, go home," a fan urged Campbell.

"I tried to avoid doing anything that would provoke the crowd," Campbell remembered. But even the act of wiping garbage off of his face inspired the crowd to greater assaults. A fan bluffed his way past an usher and punched Campbell before security dragged him away. The first period ended with Detroit leading, 4-1.

Instead of heading for cover during the intermission, Campbell remained at his seat. Soon, an angry mob descended from the upper seats and menacingly surrounded him. It was 9:11 p.m., and Miss Phyllis King, Campbell's secretary, believed the crowd was moving in for the kill. The police were too busy to protect Campbell, as they were trying to break up the riot happening outside.

At the moment of imminent doom, Campbell was unintentionally delivered to safety by a fan who hurled a tear gas bomb. It exploded about 25 feet from the commissioner and sent clouds of irritating gas wafting through the stands. People were screaming, and fourteen thousand fans stumbled for the exits.

Campbell, momentarily forgotten, escaped to the first-aid room 50 feet from his seat. Armand Pare, head of the Montreal Fire Department, refused to permit the game to continue. Campbell agreed, and Montreal forfeited the game to the Red Wings. By 11:00 p.m., more than ten thousand Montrealers and two hundred police officers were involved in the pandemonium. The Forum was under siege.

After eventually surviving the night, Campbell recalled, "I had a fine night's sleep. I was never seriously afraid of being lynched. As a referee, I learned something about mobs. They're cowards."

Unknown to Campbell, the crowd's fervor had reached demoniacal proportions soon after he left the Forum. Fifty stores in total were destroyed, and the damages reached a staggering $100,000 by 3:00 a.m., when twenty-seven people were arrested. "It's nice to have people behind you," said Richard, "but not the way they did that night." Late the next afternoon, the Rocket returned to the Forum to deliver a public statement over the radio and television.

"So that no further harm can be done," said the Rocket, "I would like to ask everyone to get behind the team and help the boys win from the Rangers and Detroit. I will take my punishment and come back next year to help the club win the Cup."

He did. He returned the following season, leading the Canadiens to first place and a Stanley Cup Championship.

18 | FIRST GOALIE TO USE A WATER BOTTLE

The image of a shot popping the bottle from the top of the net is iconic in modern hockey as a sure sign of a top-shelf goal. It was not until the 1985 Stanley Cup Final that the hydration system for the net-minders became a staple in the league. Bob Froese, the goalie for the Philadelphia Flyers, skated out and placed a water bottle on top of the net, much to the confusion of the Edmonton Oilers.

Coach Glen Sather joked about it, "What are they going to want up there next, a bucket of chicken?"

Despite the Oilers' protests, the referee allowed the bottle because Froese had secured it with Velcro, so that it would not spill and affect the ice surface.

This was the first use of a water bottle on the goalies net in the National Hockey League, but several weeks earlier, in the NCAA championship tournament, Chris Terreri and Scott Gordon both had bottles in the game.

The water bottle became commonplace in the league, and the rules changed to reflect it, stating that the bottle must be secured on top of the net.

The securing of the water bottle is not a commonly enforced rule, and many goalies now like to position the bottle to block camera views, giving them an edge in any close video reviews.

19 | HOW THE ELEPHANTS BEAT THE RANGERS—THREE IN A ROW

Madison Square Garden as we know it today actually is the fourth reincarnation of the World's Most Famous Arena.

The original structure—and its successor—was located on Madison Avenue and 26th Street across from Manhattan's famed Madison Square Park.

When MSG II was deemed obsolete, a third was erected uptown, this time on Eighth Avenue between 49th and 50th Streets. Completed in 1925, MSG III remained active until the middle of the 1967-1968 hockey season when it was replaced by the current edition sitting atop Pennsylvania Station between Seventh and Eighth Avenue and 31st and 33rd Streets.

It was Garden III that was the first to feature major league hockey games but, ironically, when the then-new arena was conceived by its designers, the ice game was a mere afterthought. Boxing and other events were the prime money-makers, but most of all it was the Ringling Brothers and Barnum and Bailey Circus that brought in the most moolah. And once the elephants came to town—which always was in the spring, at playoff time—the Rangers had to exit, stage left.

What made this such a problem for the Blueshirts was that instead of playing for the Stanley Cup before friendly home crowds, they often were compelled to compete in hostile foreign rinks. And so it was in each of the club's first three title seasons— all of the Rangers' championship victories were accomplished out-of-town.

For starters, in April 1928, the Rangers faced the heavily-favored Montreal Maroons in a best-of-five Final round. Each one of the five games was played at the Montreal Forum. Yet despite the extreme disadvantage, the Blueshirts came away with Lord Stanley's mug for the first time in the life of the franchise.

In the spring of 1933, the New Yorkers took on the Toronto Maple Leafs for The Cup and got a bit of a break. Game One was squeezed in at the Eighth Avenue arena after which the elephants galumphed into the Garden. Thus, the next three straight games were played in Maple Leaf Gardens. Despite the home ice disadvantage the Rangers prevailed, winning the tournament in four games.

Devils goalie Martin Brodeur (left) and teammate Bernie Nicholls try to thwart Rangers captain Mark Messier in the 1994 playoffs./*AP Photo/Bill Kostroun*

Toronto faced New York again in 1940, and this time the lucky Rangers were granted the first two games at home. After that the circus arrived and the remaining four games were at Maple Leaf Gardens once more. Undaunted, the Blueshirts captured the four-out-of-seven final in six games before the all-Canadian crowd.

Easily the worst—or best!—example of how the elephants beat the Rangers at Cup time occurred during the 1949-50 season when the upstart, fourth-place New Yorkers challenged the mighty Detroit Red Wings—and took them to a seventh, double-overtime game.

Before the start of that series on April 11, 1950, the circus had pushed the hockey club out of MSG, forcing coach Lynn Patrick's club to play every one of its Final Round games on the road. As a concession to the Rangers, NHL president Clarence Campbell designated that the Blueshirts could play two "home" games at Maple Leaf Gardens.

When it came time for the Finals, five of the seven games were played at Olympia Stadium in Detroit. The heroic Rangers forced a seventh game and, finally, went down on a goal by Pete Babando at 8:31 of the second sudden-death period.

By the time Garden IV was completed in 1968, high-tech ice-making equipment had been developed. It allowed for a quick change so that even though the elephants were temporarily housed in the basement of MSG, hockey games could be played at the Seventh Avenue rink if the Rangers did reach the Finals. And that explains why captain Mark Messier raised the silverware at home for the first time when the New Yorkers won their fourth Cup in 1994—whether the pachyderms liked it or not!

20 | HOW THE RANGERS TEASED GORDIE HOWE OFF THE TEAM

Before Gordie Howe belonged to any NHL club, he was nabbed by Fred McCorry for the Rangers training camp at Winnipeg the summer that Howe was fifteen years old. He arrived in the Rangers' camp, carrying a small bag that contained a shirt, set of underwear, a toothbrush, and his skates. For a young man with an outgoing personality, a sudden introduction to the NHL at the tender age of fifteen would have been a frightening experience. But to a shy, introverted teenager such as Gordie was at the time, the experience was close to shattering.

At the training table, for example, an old "pro" kept taking Gordie's plate. He was near the point of starvation when another veteran pro, defenseman Al Pike, noticed what was going on. "Hey," he called to the plate swiper, "drop that and let the kid eat." Pike later became coach of the Rangers, but eventually was fired because of his easy-going nature.

There were other embarrassments for Howe in the Rangers camp as well. For one, he did not know how to put on his equipment. "I just dropped the gear on the floor in front of me and watched the others," Gordie remembers. "I found out pretty early that the best way to learn was to keep my mouth shut and my eyes open."

But the others noticed Howe's equipment problem and teased him about it. Howe stuck it out, however, until his roommate was injured and sent home. Lonely and homesick himself, Howe fled back to Saskatoon a few days later. That winter, a scout for the Red Wings, Fred Pinckney, spotted Howe, and the following summer Gordie was invited to the Detroit training camp at Windsor, Ontario.

The Detroit boss at the time was Jack Adams, alias "Jolly Jawn," a tough hombre who could melt steel with a searing monologue, but who had an unfailing eye for hockey talent. "There was this day in Windsor, and it was the first day I ever saw him," Adams says.

"He was a big, rangy youngster who skated so easily and always seemed so perfectly balanced. It tickled me to watch him. So I called him over to the boards and said, 'What's your name son?' A lot of kids that age choke up when they start talking to you. But he just looked me in the eye and said real easy-like, 'My name's Howe.' I then remember saying, 'If you practice hard enough and try hard enough, maybe you'll make good someday.'"

Detroit signed Howe to a contract that called for a $4,000 bonus. About an hour or so after the signing, Adams found Howe standing in the hallway outside his office. He looked heartsick. "What's the matter?" Adams asked. "Well," Gordie replied, "you promised me a Red Wing jacket, but I don't have it yet."

Howe got his jacket. And the Red Wings, not the Rangers, got Gordie Howe.

21 | WORLD HOCKEY ASSOCIATION— THE LITTLE LEAGUE THAT COULD, ALMOST

During the summer of 1971, in the midst of the NHL's glorious expansion period, a *comunique* was transmitted by the national wire services about some chaps in California who hoped to create a new major hockey league in North America. What's more, Gary Davidson and Dennis Murphy, the entrepreneurs in question, were prepared to offer Phil Esposito, the Boston Bruins' scoring machine, $25,000 a year to sign with them.

The story was greeted with loud guffaws around NHL offices. Never since its birth in 1917 had the NHL ever been challenged by a brand new competitor. Oh, sure, there had been professional teams in western Canada, but they had been around as long, or longer than the NHL and rightfully challenged for the Stanley Cup. But, a new league? Never!

As it happened, the laughs heard 'round the NHL that summer of 1971 had a boomerang effect. In the end, the laugh was on the NHL for, that winter, the World Hockey Association was officially created at a meeting in New York's Americana Hotel, thereby launching one of the zaniest eras in hockey.

For some, it brought nothing by heartache. For others, it brought riches. And, for the uninvolved, it produced a million

laughs until its death in 1979. The heartache afflicted NHL officials who watched, with awe and anxiety, the component parts
of the WHA welded together and then prepare for take-off. "It,"
announced NHL president Clarence Campbell, "will never get off
the ground!"

Sage and revered, the venerable Campbell was rarely wrong.
This time he was 180 degrees off target. True, the WHA frequently
barked more than it bit, but, one by one, NHL stars expressed
an interest in the wads of $1,000 bills waved in their faces by
such previously unheard of moguls as Ben Hatskin (Winnipeg),
Howard Baldwin (Boston), and Marvin Milkes (New York).

One evening, Marty Blackman, who was involved with the
original New York WHA team, was in pursuit of a manager. He
asked a hockey writer-friend for advice. "You need a big name,"
the reporter advised. "Go for the best. Phone Rocket Richard. See
if he's interested."

Blackman got on the blower to Montreal. Hello, Maurice
Richard, would you be interested in managing the New York team
in the WHA? "What da hell," asked The Rocket, "is da WHA?"

After listening to a brief explanation, Richard said in so many
French-Canadian words, thanks-but-no-thanks, and added that
he wanted to see it to believe it. (A few years after the WHA was
born, The Rocket was hired to coach the Quebec Nordiques. He
quit after a week; it was too hard on his nerves.)

Once Bobby Hull emigrated from Chicago to Winnipeg and
signed a multi-million dollar deal with Hatskin's Jets, press
conferences sprouted all over the continent with announcements
of signings. Some NHL clubs accepted the raids with a frown, and
others fought back. One afternoon, the New York Raiders held a
media event to boast that Dave "The Hammer" Schultz and Bill
"Cowboy" Flett were about to sign with them.

Both were property of the NHL's Philadelphia Flyers; unno-
ticed, sitting in the back of the room, was Gil Stein, the Flyers'
attorney. A few weeks later, Flett and Schultz were back in
the Flyers' fold. The Boston Bruins weren't as lucky. They lost
goalie Gerry Cheevers to Cleveland and defenseman Ted Green
to the New England Whalers; not to mention Derek Sanderson to
the Philadelphia Blazers. The debut of Sanderson and the Blazers
at Philadelphia's Civic Center symbolized the future of that team.

"We couldn't play our first game," Sanderson remembered,
"because they didn't know how to make ice. It cracked wherever
we skated, so the game had to be called off." A hockey game called
because of no ice. What's next!?" In point of fact, "What's next?!"
became a veritable byword around WHA cities. The league's Los
Angeles entry, the Sharks, actually played a game at 11 a.m., which
is likely the one and only major hockey league match that ever
began before noon. It was done because of a television commit-
ment geared to prime Sunday afternoon time in the east.

Disaster seemed to be the WHA's middle name. At the start of
its second season, the league held a bizarre exhibition match at
Madison Square Garden, featuring the Golden Blades, Winnipeg
Jets, and Houston Aeros. It was Gordie Howe's first WHA appearance, and he scored a goal on his first shift. A gala press party
preceded the game, but the fate was marred by the absence of one
vital item—food.

The WHA had its share of surprises and flops. A desperate and
pathetic attempt was made to produce an effective Black Hockey
star. Thus, the opportunity came for Alton White, who played in
New York but suffered from mediocrity and never could become a
draw at the gate. He was traded by the Raiders to the Los Angeles
Sharks and, by 1974, was back in the minors.

By contrast, the biggest surprise was Ron Ward, a journey-
man NHL defenseman/forward who had played briefly for the

Toronto Maple Leafs and Vancouver Canucks before the WHA
was organized. Wats was signed by the Raiders and, by season's
end, had racked up 51 goals, playing on a line with Wayne Rivers
and Barton Bradley. Ward, overnight, had become the toast of
hockey.

He was written up in the likes of *Sports Illustrated* and treated
like a celebrity on Broadway. But before the following season had
ended, Ron had been traded three times and, after an unpleasant
tenure with the Cleveland Crusaders, called it a career. The WHA
finally cut ties with its skaters after Winnipeg defeated Edmonton
on May 20, 1979, to win the Avco World Cup, a trophy donated by
a finance company.

At the start, every WHA club had hoped to make it to the
NHL, but only four—Edmonton, Winnipeg, Quebec City, and
Hartford—did. Do you recall who *didn't*?

The Vancouver Blazers, Calgary Cowboys, Toronto Toros,
Birmingham Bulls, Ottawa Civics, New York Raiders, New York
Golden Blades, Jersey Knights, Philadelphia Blazers, Baltimore
Blades, Cleveland Crusaders, Michigan Stags, Chicago Cougars,
Indianapolis Racers, Cincinnati Stingers, Miami Screaming Eagles,
Houston Aeros, Minnesota Fighting Saints, Denver Spurs, Phoenix
Roadrunners, San Diego Mariners, and Los Angeles Sharks.

22 | THE STRANGE TRAVELS OF THE STANLEY CUP

The Stanley Cup is easily one of the most treasured trophies in the entire sports world. Yet, its life has been filled with irony and contradictions. Incredibly, the Cup wasn't originally meant to be awarded to the champions of professional hockey. It was intended to be presented to the leading amateurs of Canada.

Even more ironic, the man after whom it was named—Lord Stanley of Preston, Canada's governor-general—really didn't give a damn about hockey. His son, Arthur Stanley, was the hockey buff in the family, and he, along with his aide, Lord Kilcoursie, and Ottawa publisher P. D. Ross, persuaded Lord Stanley to purchase the silver mug in 1893 and award it to the leading amateur team.

The Cup, valued then at $48.67, was first won by the Montreal Amateur Athletic Association. It remained in the amateur ranks until 1912, when it was captured by a professional team, the Quebec Bulldogs. If Sir Arthur Conan Doyle had spent his writing years in Canada, there's every reason to believe he'd have penned a few adventures of Sherlock Holmes and the Stanley Cup. One of the earliest and best cup stories occurred in 1905 after the Ottawa Silver Screen had won the cup.

Jubilant Ottawa fans had presented their champs with a gala victory dinner that sent many of the victors well into the grape. Finally the party ended and the Ottawa skaters stumbled home in the bitter cold of the night. As refreshing as the Arctic air may have been, it wasn't enough to clear the mind of Harry Smith, a stalwart of the Silver Seven.

Through Harry's somewhat distorted eyes, the revered cup took on all the aspects of a football. He grabbed the trophy and delivered a perfect place-kick that sent the cup arching into the Rideau Canal. Since the other troops were no more sober than Smith, the Cup remained in the Rideau, and the Silver Seven headed home. The next morning, Harry Smith began to suspect that he had been guilty of a rather rash placekick.

He dressed quickly, dashed back to the Rideau Canal, and there he found the Cup, nestled in the bone-dry bed. The dents that Harry's boot had put in the Cup weren't to be his last. A year later, the Montreal Wanderers captured the championship and proudly hauled the Cup to the studio of a photographer named Jimmy Rice. There they proudly lined up for the traditional victory portrait, with the Stanley Cup standing before the victorious Wanderers.

When Jimmy Rice gave the final click of the shutter, the Wanderers gleefully filed out of the studio for the nearest pub. Perhaps the visions of malt hops were dancing in their heads. Whatever it was, the Wanderers jubilantly departed and never gave a thought to the trophy.

In fact, nobody but a charwoman was concerned about the Cup. When the last of the Wanderers had left the studio, the cleaning lady noticed the interesting silver cup sitting on the floor. "My," she must have said, "but this would make a lovely flower spot." So she took the Stanley Cup home.

Several months later, the Wanderer's management thought it would be a noble gesture if the Stanley Cup were placed on display in the victors' arena. But, alas, where was the trophy? The last place anyone remembered seeing it was at Jimmy Rice's studio. Jimmy was contacted. He called his charwoman, who explained that the Stanley Cup was on her mantel—literally in full bloom.

In 1924, when the Montreal Canadiens captured the Cup, they were feted by the University of Montreal in a public reception at the National Monument in Montreal. After the reception, the Canadiens were invited by the team's owner, Leo Dandurand, to a party at his home. Before they got there, the Cup managed to escape again. According to Dandurand, here's how it happened:

"Georges Vezina, Sprague Cleghorn, Sylvio Mantha, and I got into a Model T Ford to make the trip. The little lizzie stalled going up Cote St. Antoine Road in Westmount, and we all got out to push. Cleghorn, who had been jealously carrying the cup in his lap, deposited it on the curb at roadside before he joined us in shoving the car up the hill. When we reached the top, we hopped back into the car and resumed our hockey chatter as we got going again.

"Upon reaching my house, we all started in on a big bowl of punch my wife had prepared. It wasn't until she asked, 'Well, where is the Stanley Cup you've been talking about?' that we realized Cleghorn had left it on the side of the road. Sprague and I drove hurriedly back to the spot almost an hour after we had pushed the car up the hill. There was the Cup, in all its shining majesty, still sitting on the curb of the busy street."

During the playoffs of April 1962, the Cup resided in a huge glass case right in the midst of the Chicago Stadium lobby for all to see. The Blackhawks had won the world championship the previous year and were now engaged in another furious battle for the trophy.

A Montreal fan by the name of Ken Kilander took a dim view of the Stanley Cup's residing in Chicago. He studied the silver mug and the glass case with the intensity of a safecracker about to launch a great heist. The temptation proved too much for him, so he did it. He opened the glass case and when, to his supreme amazement, neither gongs nor sirens nor any form of a warning buzzer sounded, he gingerly reached in and plucked the Cup off it stand.

Still not a sound. There was just one thing to do, leave. Nursing the Cup with affection, Kilander headed to the exit doors. It was almost too good to be true.

He was just a few yards from freedom when a cop spotted him and asked why he happened to be carrying the Stanley Cup out of Chicago Stadium. Kilander's retort will never win him entrance into Bartlett's *Familiar Quotations*, abridged or unabridged, but it might get him a prize for sincerity.

"I want to take it back to where it belongs. In Montreal."

Being a Chicagoan, the cop disagreed. He returned the Cup to the glass case where it belonged, and Kilander was urged to permit Cup movements to be decided on the ice.

23 | HOW THE DUCKS CREATED AN NHL TEAM ON LONG ISLAND

Among its outstanding attractions, Long Island is famous for its beaches, its estates, and its production of ducks, the eating kind.

Long Island ducks had become so popular in the late 1960s that a minor league hockey team in Commack, New York, was named after them.

However, the Ducks not only turned into a popular hockey club. Remarkably, they helped create an NHL team in Nassau County.

This remarkable feat began with a Long Island contractor named Al Baron, who bought the Ducks and supported them at the Long Island Arena.

Although he owned the club, Baron also was its biggest fan and even went so far as to broadcast some of its games. At one point, he purchased a twin-engined Douglas DC-3 for his team and flew them to Eastern League games in class.

More than anything, the Ducks became a hit on the Island because they provided fans with good pucks for their bucks. Games were entertaining, and the tickets were cheap. What's more, Long Island Arena boasted an ambience of a small-town western Canadian rink.

There was no glass—or any protection for that matter—along the sideboards which enabled Ducks fans to occasionally deliver a whack to the backside of visiting players. The barn-like building was like one large social hall, with almost everyone knowing everyone else. And that included the players.

Baron ensured that he had a colorful team. Burly defensemen such as Ray Crew and Don Perry were already Eastern League legends by the time they reached Commack, and another backliner, John Brophy, became such an institution that the Paul Newman role in the classic film *Slapshot* was patterned after him.

NHL stars such as Ed Giacomin and Gilles Villemure played for the Ducks as well as top-grade minor leaguers such as Buzz Deschamps, Norm Ryder, Don Atamanchuk, and Gene Achtymichuk, among many others.

In many ways, the Ducks saga followed the storyline of *Slapshot*. Games would occasionally erupt into a riot on the ice, and visiting teams were often subject to abuse above and beyond the call of duty. But the spirited atmosphere suited the suburbanites, and the Ducks established Long Island as a minor pro hockey hotbed. In fact, they may have done so at their own expense.

When the lords of Nassau County decided to build an arena on the Hempstead Plain within view of the Mitchell Field hangers from where Charles Lindbergh took off for Paris, they chose to make it major league size. That meant a big-league team would be necessary or, at the very least, a top minor league club. In either case, it would be competition for the Ducks.

"I was interested in getting involved in whatever hockey club they had planned for the new building," said Baron. "I had a right to want to be there, since my Ducks had created all the fans that would be going to the big arena."

Unfortunately, Al did not get his wish. While true that the Ducks created intense hockey interest on Long Island, the good word was never reciprocated by the NHL.

Once the Islanders took hold, the minor league franchise in Commack was doomed, and while the new big-league club at Nassau Coliseum was to thrive, the team at Long Island Arena that made it all possible passed into hockey oblivion.

24 | HOW A WALK AROUND THE BLOCK SAVED THE ISLANDERS FRANCHISE

If any player made the Islanders a four-Stanley Cup dynasty, it was Hall of Fame defenseman Denis Potvin. But were it not for a walk around the block in Montreal, Potvin may never have become an Islander and the Nassau franchise might never have had a championship to its name.

It all happened as a result of the Isles' last-place finish in their first year in the NHL, 1972-73. This meant that the club's general manager Bill Torrey would have first pick in the entry draft. And naturally, Denis Potvin was there for the plucking.

Quite often, junior prospects are more the product of press clippings than substance, but everyone knew that Potvin was the real goods. And nobody knew that better than Montreal Canadiens general manager Sammy Pollock, the presiding genius among his colleagues. Pollock liked Potvin as much as he liked to breathe and determined that he would do everything short of kidnapping to obtain the prodigy.

Torrey, who never talked to hockey people with his eyes closed, knew precisely what Pollock's strategy would be and went about the business of blunting it. To do so, Torrey had to practice saying, No. No. A thousand times NO!" whenever Pollock made a pitch for Potvin.

Pollock hounded Torrey before the actual draft—they took a long walk around the block in Montreal—at the Queen Elizabeth Hotel and even tried an eleventh-and-a-half hour deal before Torrey made his pick. Pollock was prepared to offer four good NHL players for the kid and, for a moment, it appeared that the Isles boss might relent.

"This much I know," said Potvin. "I was there, and when I saw Pollock's last move, I thought he had finally convinced Bill to send me to Montreal."

Wrong. Torrey let his wits hold forth and selected the 6'0", 205-pound defenseman who had the confidence and ego of a veteran. When reporters compared him to Bobby Orr, Potvin responded that, no, he would not be a second Bobby Orr but rather the first Denis Potvin. Period.

He was right on that count. Orr won two Stanley Cups in his career, while Potvin had a quartet, and in the eyes of some experts could be rated the best all-around defenseman of all-time—all because of Bill Torrey's long walk.

25 | SANTA'S FAVORITE HOCKEY TEAM

Once upon a time when the NHL was a six-team league, it was traditional for teams to play on Christmas night. Of all the clubs that played on Christmas, none had better connections with Santa Claus than the New York Rangers. It was a matter of sheer luck, but the Broadway Blueshirts didn't complain.

During the period between 1928 and 1950, the Rangers went undefeated in 14 of their Yule night contests, including a string of nine straight. They finally fell from the graces of St. Nick on Christmas night 1950, when the New Yorkers were defeated by the Red Wings in Detroit. The only other blemish on their record during this time came at the hands of the Chicago Blackhawks, a 3-3 overtime tie in 1940.

A true test of the Rangers' Christmas magic came during the 1943-44 season. Decimated by the wartime man-power shortage, the New Yorkers managed only six victories out of a 50-game schedule. But of the six, one was found under the Christmas tree, a 5-3 win over Toronto in Maple Leaf Gardens, of all places. The win fired them up so much that they went home and beat the Blackhawks the following night, 7-6, completing their longest winning streak of the season.

Ironically, the Rangers' first home ice loss on Christmas since 1928 came during the 1957-58 season when they finished second, their best showing of the post-war years. The culprits this time were the Blackhawks, who beat the Blueshirts 3-1.

But although the Rangers enjoyed such great success on Christmas night, it was their loss in 1928 that will perhaps be best remembered. Besides being a holiday contest, it was a grudge match against their intra-city rivals, the New York Americans.

For a game of such importance, Rangers president Colonel John S. Hammond made a special request to league president Frank Calder, asking for the best referee available to handle the contest. President Calder complied, dispatching his best whistleblower, assuring Colonel Hammond that there would indeed be extraordinary attention paid to the officiating of the game. The referee in question was one Billy Bell, a chap with a reputation for calling them as he saw them *instead of the way they actually happened.*

Bell's style was obvious from the opening faceoff. The first goal of the game was apparently scored by Rangers right wing Bill Cook. He blasted a shot into the net, whereupon his momentum carried him into Amerks' goalie Roy (Shrimp) Worters. The puck had already crossed the goal line. What was obvious to everyone in the Garden was right next to Billy Bell. He gave the wash-out motion, signifying no goal, and explained: "Cook was in the crease when he shot."

After the uproar had subsided, the game settled into a score-less battle until, with four minutes left in the third period, Bell again took the game into his own hands. He claimed that a shot by Americans' forward Rabbit McVeigh had hit the inside of the cage and bounced quickly out.

This vision of a score had eluded everyone, including the goal judge, whose moniker was "Big Nose Harry." In the face of raging protests by the Rangers, Bell stuck to his guns, and the Americans led, 1-0.

The Rangers were certainly furious, but they were far from done. They fought on until, at the 18:00 mark Murray "Mudhooks" Murdoch drilled one behind Worters. But as quickly as the Rangers could lift their sticks with joy, Bell brought them down again. Indicating that Murdoch had been offsides, he again ruled "no goal!"

Not surprisingly, after the game Bell was escorted to the referee's dressing room by a police guard to avoid the impromptu lynch mob of Rangers fans who were militantly unhappy with Bell's performance. But "Big Nose Harry" didn't fare as well. While he was comparatively innocent of poor judgment on the American goal, he was nonetheless involved in the controversy.

In those days, there was no herculite glass surrounding the rink, only a wire arrangement that allowed just enough of an opening for a well-aimed butt-end to penetrate. It seems as though Harry's nose wandered a bit too close to an aperture in the chicken wire, where he caught that well-aimed butt squarely in the snoot. The culprit remains anonymous to this day, but the shot left Harry's nose closely resembling that of a Proboscis Monkey.

But even though the Grinch stole their Christmas in 1928, the Rangers fared far better in the following years.

In 1961, Christmas baby Larry Cahan celebrated his birthday by scoring the game winner in a 6-4 win over the Red Wings, the Rangers' chief rivals for the last qualifying playoff position.

Hall of Famer Harry Howell, in recalling that particular triumph, was asked if there were any grim Christmas nights in his Rangers history. He replied that on one holiday, the team arrived in Montreal late in the evening and found not a restaurant, diner, nor even a cafeteria open. The Rangers had to endure a hunger-stricken night before their game against the Habs. Reliving the uncomfortable day, Harry lamented, "Then we got put on the ice and got the pants beat off us. Some Christmas!"

II
Colorful
Characters

26 | THE SWEET ALL-AMERICA "DOCTOR" TURNS SOUR GOON

There are all kinds of doctors. You can start with medical doctors, shrinks, and those who live in Ivory towers; otherwise known as PhDs.

In the National Hockey League there have been two distinct species of docs—the ones who tend to wounds and the one who skated for the Chicago Blackhawks.

Elwyn (Doc) Romnes—out of White Bear Lake, Minnesota— was a slick center who just hated his given name but loved being called Doc. However, he was neither medic, psychiatrist, nor Doctor of Philosophy. Elwyn got the monicker because he carried his skates in a physician's case, of all places to keep the blades.

Even more fascinating is the fact that in December 1930 Romnes became the first Minnesotan to play in the National Hockey League. That didn't impress his teammates, though, all of whom were Canadian lads. In those parochial NHL days, an American-born player was treated with less admiration than had he just been traded to Chicago from Devils Island.

"There were times," Romnes recalled, "when nobody on my own Blackhawks team talked to me. They treated me a little like I was a thief. The Canadians wondered what an American was doing invading their preserve. That's why I became a good playmaker, setting those fellows up so they'd talk to me. I eventually got accepted, but it wasn't easy."

What made acceptance less difficult were Doc's assortment of skills, some of which enabled Chicago to win its first Stanley Cup in 1934. As a result, Romnes became the first Minnesotan to have his name on the silverware. A year later, he won the Lady Byng Trophy for good sportsmanship and competent play.

But in 1938, for a brief moment, Doc turned aggressive on the ice. Either Romnes completely lost his marbles or was so bent on achieving justice, but he simply couldn't contain his fury. This much is certain, though, he picked the wrong guy with whom to mess.

Even when he was in a good mood, George Reginald (Red) Horner was not a man to be trifled with and played a game that was one of the most physical in the NHL at the time.

Romnes, who later was inducted into the United States Hockey Hall of Fame, insisted that he never would have acted so completely out of character under normal circumstances. But he had been so unabashedly brutalized by the Toronto Maple Leafs defenseman during the 1938 Stanley Cup Final between the Blackhawks and Maple Leafs, the Doctor had no choice but to perform surgery on The Redhead with a wooden stick instead of a scalpel.

"In our first game against the Leafs," Romnes explained, "Horner broke my nose in five places. That game was played at Maple Leaf Gardens. I told Red I'd get him in Chicago. Some people thought that my coach, Bill Stewart, had something to do with my plan of retaliation, but that wasn't true. It was all my idea.

"When the second game was ready to start, I was out for the faceoff. I skated up to Horner and swung my stick at his head.

Remember, I wasn't that kind of player, but in this particular instance I went berserk."

Once the ice had cleared and the penalties meted out, the teams settled down to hockey and eventually the Blackhawks went on to win their second Stanley Cup by beating the Leafs.

Despite the fact that he seemingly "got even" with Horner, Doc's hatred for the Toronto enforcer did not abate with the head-knocking at center ice. Every time he faced the Royal Blue and White fellows, Romnes kept an Argus eye out for his nemesis. And then it happened.

Doc, who never in his wildest dreams—or nightmares—could imagine himself playing on the same team as Horner, was traded to the Maple Leafs.

Romnes: "We were on our first road trip of the season after we'd won the Stanley Cup. On our way home from Boston, our manager, Bill Tobin, sent me word I'd been traded to Toronto. That meant Horner and I would be teammates. When the train reached Buffalo, I got off and headed for Chicago. I informed Tobin that I was through.

"Back in Chicago, Tobin sent a taxi and asked me down to the office. There was a bonus clause in my contract that stipulated I would be paid $1,500 if I scored a certain number of goals. Tobin told me the bonus would be waiting for me in Toronto if I would report. Well, I couldn't afford to lose $1,500, so I went."

During his journey to Toronto, it was only natural for Doc to puzzle over the move. He questioned whether or not he could co-exist on the same team as Horner, particularly in view of their heated clashes. But when Romnes arrived at the Canadian National Terminal in Toronto, he was in for a pleasant—call it stunning—surprise.

"When I got off the train," Doc remembered, "the first person I saw was Red Horner. I didn't know what to think, but Red removed all my misgivings in a moment. He said: 'C'mon, Doc, from now on you and I are on the same side.' He turned out to be a terrific guy!"

Then again, the Redhead allowed that the vice was versa. Romnes was truly the good Doc.

27 | HOW AN NHL PLAYER CREATED A NEW RULE

Few players have been surrounded in as much controversy as Sean Avery was during his ten-year National Hockey League career.

In the 2008 Eastern Conference Quarterfinals, Avery's Rangers had a five-on-three power play against the New Jersey Devils. When the power play began, Avery made his way to the front of the Devils net and near New Jersey's legendary netminder Martin Brodeur.

What happened next was never seen before in the NHL. The Rangers agitator faced Brodeur, waving his arms and stick in an attempt to distract the Devils goalie. The scene drew the ire of the Devils on the ice, as well as referee Don Van Massenhoven, who threatened to give Avery a penalty.

The puck was eventually cleared out of the zone, but when the Blueshirts stormed back into New Jersey's end, Avery scored to give the Rangers a 2-1 lead.

The day after the incident, the NHL created a new rule, stating that distracting the goalie in such a manner would result in a minor penalty for unsportsmanlike conduct.

As a New York Rangers forward, Sean Avery was notorious for being a super pest on the ice while working in the fashion industry during the off-season./ *David Perlmutter*

Ever since then, goalie distraction in that manner is known as The Sean Avery Rule; no other NHLer before or since could make that statement.

And that in itself is an incredible feat.

28 | HOW TO TURN SUPERSTITIONS INTO A WIN

When George "Punch" Imlach coached the Toronto Maple Leafs, they won three straight Stanley Cups—1962, 1963, 1964—plus a fourth in 1967. Imlach's superstitions ranged from the fedoras he wore behind the Toronto bench or assorted other pieces of apparel.

It was said that over the decades, Imlach was among the most superstitious of hockey people ever since he played for the old Quebec Aces of the Quebec Senior Hockey League. During one series, he bought a new suit each time he brought the Maple Leafs to Montreal's Forum.

"Will it help?" someone asked Punch.

"Sure," Imlach replied, "if my goalie is good and we score a lot of goals!"

29 | THE GAYE STEWART KISS IN THE GARDEN

Before the advent of Hercultie glass surrounding the ice surface, players were sometimes chucked over the boards and into the laps of fans. During a game at Madison Square Garden in the 1950s, Gaye Stewart of the Rangers was dumped over the boards by Ernie Dickens of the Blackhawks and right into the lap of a portly gentleman drinking beer.

Seated next to the man was a lovely young woman who was shocked to find a player next to her. The beer went one way, and Stewart, always with an eye for beauty, gallantly planted a kiss on the young lady's cheek, gently helped the man from the floor and, reeking with the aroma of spilled beer, hurdled the boards and resumed play!

Some of us in the press box suggested that the LEAST Stewart could have done was order ANOTHER beer for the fan!

30 | PETTY CASH

Decades ago, in the era that preceded agents, attorneys, and six-figure salaries for untried rookies, it was not uncommon for big-league managers to trim the budgets of their freshman skaters to the bone. One of the tightest of these front office types was William J. (Bill) Tobin, who managed the Chicago Blackhawks in the late 1930s and 1940s.

"The expense account allowance," Tobin once explained, "gave the boys a chance to imagine they were adult big leaguers and they did some of the darndest things." Tobin had figured that he had seen everything until one day a lad approached him after five days of training camp and said, "Mister Tobin, it's cost me a little extra above the club's allowance to live here, and I'd like something to cover my expenses."

Tobin anticipated a rather inflated figure and inquired how much the youngster had in mind. "Just $10.35," he replied.

The unusual figure piqued Tobin's interest. "It's all right about the ten dollars," said Tobin, "but how do you figure it right down to 35 cents?

The youngster retorted with a perfectly straight face: "It'll cost me 35 cents to send a telegram to my Dad to tell him I got the ten dollars!"

Because the Blackhawks were not playing to capacity crowds in those Depression Era days, Tobin was forced to be frugal above and beyond the call of duty. Once, this behavior reduced him to crawling around on his hands and knees, looking for a Blackhawks player's front teeth.

It happened after a game at Chicago Stadium when Black Hawk's defenseman Virgil Johnson ran up to Tobin and, in a state of high anguish, shouted: "Mister Tobin, I've lost my teeth! That bridgework in front was jarred loose in the last minute of play, and I can't find it on the ice."

Tobin remembered that the Blackhawks had bought the teeth for Johnson—and they were very expensive. The manager asked Johnson to point out the spot where he believed the teeth had fallen, and they began searching.

"I looked for it where slush is drained off the floor when the ice is being removed," said Tobin, "and told one of the workmen what happened and how important it was that we got those teeth. The fellow grabbed a window screen lying on the floor nearby and held it under the spout. Before long, out squirted the truant teeth.

"All they needed was a little tap-water, some brushing up, and they were as good as ever. I had saved the club a few precious bucks in the process."

Like all fiscally sound general managers, Tobin insisted that his players submit expense accounts for purchases made with the team's money. Among his favorites was one submitted by a rookie. It read as follows: "One sack of apples; one detective story magazine; one pair of shoelaces for dress shoes; one box (small) of Epsom salts."

Tobin suffered his share of contract disputes, but the most perplexing reply he ever received came from a sophomore who had completed a successful rookie season and demanded a hefty raise, far beyond Tobin's budget. The bickering went on for several weeks and finally caught the attention of the newspapers, whereupon the player dispatched the following wire to Tobin:

"DEAR BILL: SEE BY PAPERS I AM HOLDOUT. I AM NOT HOLDOUT BUT LIKE TO PLAY HOCKEY FOR YOU. HOWEVER I WILL NOT SIGN CONTRACT UNLESS I AM PAID MORE MONEY."

31 | HOW LYNN PATRICK REGAINED A ROSTER SPOT WHEN HIS FATHER, THE G.M., SAID NO

While his father, Lester Patrick, was president and general manager of the Rangers during the late 1930s, his older son Lynn and younger son Murray (Muzz) played left wing and defense, respectively. Both starred on the 1940 Stanley Cup-winning New York team. And when America entered World War II, the young Patricks enlisted in the U.S. Army.

Like many National Hockey League enlistees, the Patricks lost much of their hockey skills by the end of the war. Several Rangers, such as captain Art Coulter, who had played on the Cup-winning team, realized that their legs "were gone" and simply retired. Many believed that Lynn Patrick no longer belonged in hockey's major league, and when Lynn was discharged from the army, his father told him that he would not be welcome on the Rangers roster.

Since Lester was acknowledged as the total boss of New York hockey, it appeared that Lynn would have to take a job in the minors as a player or simply retire and turn to coaching. But Lynn challenged his Old Man and said that he believed that he was good enough to make the big team. However, Lester would not bend, and everyone at Madison Square Garden knew that The

Silver Fox always had the last word when it came to the Rangers roster.

So, how then did Lynn Patrick top Lester Patrick on this career-turning challenge?

During World War II, the government in Washington took into account the needs of servicemen once the conflict had ended. A product of that thinking was called "The GI Bill of Rights," and among its stipulations was that any serviceman who had a job before the war was entitled to get that very same employment back.

Presented with the GI Bill, the patriotic Lester had no choice but to re-hire—against his will—his ex-GI son Lynn and, sure enough, when the 1945-46 season began, Lynn returned to his spot on left wing. What's more, Lynn proved his father at least partially wrong. Over a spate of 38 games, he produced eight goals and six assists for 14 points, which wasn't bad from a skater whose legs supposedly were "gone."

Lester didn't make a fuss over Muzz's return. He allowed the younger Patrick to try his luck on defense. In 23 games, Muzz scored nothing and had two assists.

By the end of the season, the brothers retired and went into coaching, but at least Lynn had the satisfaction of knowing that the GI Bill could get him his hockey job back; at least for one more season!

32 | HOW A BULLET BECOMES A CORKSCREW IN ONE EASY LESSON

National Hockey League star Joe Simpson was originally nicknamed "Bullet Joe." However, Simpson eventually wound up on Broadway playing for the New York Americans. The Amerks' manager, Tommy Gorman, was impressed with the manner in which Simpson carried the puck. He would skate rapidly on a twisting route. After watching him a few times, Gorman described the forays as "corkscrew rushes." Hence, "Corkscrew Joe."

33 | TURNABOUT IS FAIR PLAY

Steve Sullivan of the Chicago Blackhawks thought it was "bloody awful" after being high-sticked by his own teammate. Adding insult to his injury, the miniscule forward

Steve Sullivan—shown here as a member of the Nashville Predators—suffered some of the strangest injuries during his long NHL career./*AP Photo/Nam Y. Huh*

found himself being heckled by a fan who found the bloody Sully's face a source of amusement.

Filing the fan's face in his memory bank, the injured center went off for repairs. Little did he realize that revenge would come in a most curious and satisfying way.

Karma seemed to be working overtime that night, and due to an incredibly improbable turn of events, the very same fan was struck in the head by a puck later on in the game. Sullivan seized the opportunity to remind the irate fan that what goes around, comes around!

What's more, the Hawks' alternate captain went on to score the only two Chicago goals of the night—both shorthanded—literally adding insult to injury. Though the Avalanche fan was undoubtedly pleased by his team's 5-2 victory, suffice it to say that Steve Sullivan had the last laugh.

34 | FROM THE PENALTY BOX TO THE PULPIT

Lester John Thomas Costello was a battler; "a tough little bugger," as his former coach Baz Bastien put it. Those who observed him during his playing days with the Toronto Maple Leafs of the NHL and the Pittsburgh Hornets of the AHL remember him as a scrappy player and a fun-loving prankster. Little did his hockey colleagues realize that his playing days were just a stopover on his way to quite a different career with a very different image. Reverend Les Costello, pastor of the Blessed Sacrament Parish in Noranada, Quebec, was quite a shock to the hockey world.

"He is the last guy in the world you would have figured would have become a priest," said one AHL official. Fleming Mackell, Costello's erstwhile linemate while with the Hornets, recalled Les' less-than-holy-hell-raising in his playing days.

"There may have been better players than Les Costello," said Mackell, "but none with more fire and determination. Later, when we were with Pittsburgh, Cos made it his business to get even with Ott Heller one night. Ott was playing-coach at Indianapolis in those days, and he seemed to take pleasure in giving us young kids a lot of stiff bodychecks. Well, that night, Cos really gave him a taste of his own medicine, and Heller didn't bother us much after that."

The 5-9, 160-pound left winger ended his short hockey career at the age of twenty-three. He had skated for three years with Pittsburgh and part of one season with the Maple Leafs. "I could have continued to play in the NHL," said Father Les, "but I had a strong inclination to go into the priesthood. I guess that was my call in life."

Father Les was ordained in 1957 and was originally assigned pastor of the Holy Name Parish in Kirkland Lake, Ontario, the home town of Detroit Red Wing's bad boy, Ted Lindsay. Lindsay, like Costello, was a tough little competitor when he skated for the Wings.

"I'll admit though," says Father Les, "that overall the players of today are better than they were 15 years ago." Costello was referring to "youngsters" such as Henri Richard and Dave Keon.

"Fleming Mackell and I were playing together on a line with Max Bentley when Toronto owner Conn Smythe called us into his office," remembered Father Les. "I knew that he was going to send either Fleming or myself down to Pittsburgh, and we both felt that I was the one who was getting the train ticket.

"Mr. Smythe told us that our line wasn't going too well defensively. With this, Mackell got angry and sort of told Mr. Smythe off. As you probably can guess, Fleming wound up with the ticket to Pittsburgh. I really put the razz on him after that one. But I wasn't laughing for long; I wound up in Pittsburgh two weeks later."

Hockey has held some great thrills for Father Les Costello, such as his first goal in the NHL during the 1947-48 campaign. "I scored a goal the first time I got on the ice," he said. "I took a pass from Max Bentley and shot the puck past Frank 'Mr. Zero' Brimsek in the Boston net. But on the next shift I got a penalty.

We beat the Bruins in the semi-finals and won the Cup by beating the Red Wings. I scored one goal against Detroit."

The goals scored and great players he faced are thoroughly entrenched in his memory, but Father Costello was called away for a career with results at least as rewarding as winning the Stanley Cup.

35 | HAP DAY AND WALTER PRATT

One of the most rambunctious players of all-time was a fellow named Walter "Babe" Pratt, who starred for the New York Rangers and later the Toronto Maple Leafs.

On each team, Pratt had his problems with management simply because he liked to drink; and we aren't talking about seltzer either.

"It seemed like every time Lester Patrick walked into a [bar] room," Pratt recalled, "especially during the playoffs I wouldn't necessarily be drinking, but I would be there. I would always get caught. Somebody else could be drinking away in another hotel or pub, but Lester always managed to find me. It seemed to me at the time that I wasn't doing any harm, but Lester used to make it a lot worse than it was and I used to go along with it as a gag. A couple of times he chastised me, and he caught me on more serious things. One time, he said, 'I'm not going to fine you, I'm not going to trade you, I'm going to send you down to the minors until you rot!'"

Pratt laughed because he was sure Lester would never go through with his threat, knowing that Pratt could play for any team in the league. "He finally wound up fining me $1,000, a fantastic sum when you're only making about $5,000 for the year.

He kept it for one month, but I was playing so well he felt guilty and gave it back."

Babe and Lester didn't always get along, especially when money was the subject. According to Pratt, Patrick wasn't tight with money, "He was adjacent to it!" Lester finally traded Babe to Toronto in 1942, and to Pratt's astonishment he was paid more by the Leafs than Lester ever paid him. As a result, he began to play even better. When Lester found out about Pratt's good fortune, he asked Babe about it.

"Lester," Pratt explained, "Now I'm being paid enough to eat on. I'm finally getting the wrinkles out of my belly."

Once Pratt was traded to Toronto, the Maple Leafs' version of Patrick was Clerence "Hap" Day, the Toronto coach.

Like Patrick, Day's challenge was finding ways and means to keep Babe away from the booze. One day Hap came up with an idea: he could keep Pratt on the straight and narrow only if his star player was close by at all times. So Day and Pratt became roommates. "It was the worst time of my life," Pratt said of the sleeping arrangement, "because we were awake until four in the morning while he talked hockey. I'd scream at him, 'Jesus, I could be out drinking and here we are talking hockey!' that used to make him mad and he'd say 'if you laid off that stuff you'd have been the greatest hockey player who ever lived.' Every time I've ever had to call him in later years he'd say 'hello' and I'd say, 'this is the greatest,' and he knew who it was immediately."

Pratt readily admitted that Day was the "greatest coach in hockey," but he didn't have too much fun when Hap was around. "He wasn't a very complimentary guy," Babe recalled. "If you bumped into him in the street, he'd say 'Nice pass you made in Chicago,' and that would mean that you gave the puck away."

But if ever Day got to like his gifted defenseman it was in the 1945 Stanley Cup finals between the Leafs and Red Wings.

The series went to a seventh game, which was played at Detroit's Olympia stadium on April 22, 1945. The Leafs took the lead 1-0 on a goal by Mel Hill, but Murray Armstrong of Detroit tied the count at 1-1 with a goal at 8:16 of the third period.

When the Red Wings took a penalty midway in the third stanza, The Babe took center stage and scored for Toronto at 12:14. It was the cup-winning goal, as the Maple Leafs took the match 2-1.

Perhaps as amusing as anything is Pratt's recollection of what transpired that afternoon and evening in the Motor City.

"I'll always remember the final game in Detroit when we won the Stanley Cup and I scored the winning goal. Before the game started, Hap paced around the living room of the suite while I was snoring in bed. He came in and dumped me right out of bed and yelled 'How the hell can you lay there and snore before the seventh game of the Stanley Cup finals?' I said, 'Well, the game doesn't start for another hour. There's no use me doing any worrying until then. That's your job."

In the end, both The Babe and Hap did their jobs very well; especially when Pratt was on the ice and not in a tavern!

36 | HOW CHING JOHNSON WAS UN-AMERICAN TO THE AMERICANS

Hall of Famer Ivan "Ching" Johnson was an original New York Rangers defenseman. Signed in 1926, Johnson played a full ten years on the Blueshirts' backline. But in 1937, Ching was dealt to the Blueshirts' rival at Madison Square Garden, the New York Americans.

This was a shocker for New York hockey fans, since Johnson was as associated with the Rangers as Broadway is with Times Square. The Garden was sold out the first night that Ching lined up with the Americans against his former teammates.

Joseph Nichols, who covered that game for *The New York Times*, remembered a bizarre episode that soon would take place.

In a nutshell, Johnson did something peculiarly un-American to his new team, the Americans. "The whole town was pulling for Ching," wrote Nichols, "and Johnson responded by seizing the puck on one occasion, skating furiously in all directions, and letting fly with a sharp shot that eluded Earl Robertson and landed in the net.

"The smile that suffused Johnson's face at this effort was suddenly erased, though, when the realization struck home that Robertson was the goalie for the Americans—Ching's own team!"

PS: Johnson went on to redeem himself for the Amerks. He helped them to a rare playoff berth, and in the first round they eliminated the Rangers from the postseason, in a game that went four overtimes at the Garden. For Ching, it was sweet revenge.

37 | THE HOCKEY PLAYER WHO SERVED AS THE TEAM CLOWN

When **Wally Stanowski** was traded from the Toronto Maple Leafs to the New York Rangers in the late 1940s, he sharpened his already famous wit by taunting his own teammates. Veteran New York hockey reporters tell about the times when Wally would walk down Forty-Ninth Street (site of the old Madison Square Garden) and pass by the Rangers' dressing room that frequently had the upper transom partially opened.

Disguising his voice as that of an anonymous fan, Stanowski would single out one of his teammates and berate him with deep purple language. Then, he would continue into the dressing room and innocently sit down at his bench and dress, occasionally snickering at one of his teammates who was in on the prank.

"I used to fool around. I liked going in to magic shops to buy trick cards; anything to entertain my teammates. Anything for a couple of laughs."

Once he was on the ice, Stanowski discarded his sense of humor. Especially when he faced the likes of Maurice Richard. "There's no doubt," Wally concluded, "that Richard was the toughest person for me to defend against. He was a very powerful skater and very difficult to knock off his feet. His physical strength was immense. He was the hardest player to stop. Period."

Stanowski lives in Toronto, where at the age of ninety-four, he is the oldest living member of four Stanley Cup-winning Toronto Maple Leaf teams. And if that isn't incredible enough, what is?

38 | THE HOCKEY-INTENSE MAYOR OF NEW YORK CITY

Gentleman mayor Jimmy Walker, New York City's most dashing, debonair mayor, is better remembered for his political machinations, Broadway dash, and musical compositions than his affiliations with hockey.

But, Jimmy, with his showbiz style, loved sports and hockey in particular.

In the fall of 1926 when the Metropolitan Amateur Hockey Association was organized, Mayor Walker presented a trophy bearing his name to the Knickerbockers, but the league was disbanded the following season.

Through the efforts of General John Reed Kilpatrick, president of Madison Square Garden, the Walker Trophy was placed in competition in 1933 in the Eastern League. The Atlantic City Sea Gulls were the first EHL winners in 1933-34.

Like its NHL counterpart, the Stanley Cup, the Walker Trophy had a zany life. Once, it was stolen from its Madison Square Garden showcase and a reward was posted. A few days later, it was discovered sitting in a window of a nearby Eighth Avenue pawnshop.

A Garden official retrieved it and the Walker Trophy was placed back into competition. During the 1946-47 season, the year Jimmy Walker died, the trophy was captured by the New York Rovers, his favorite team.

39 | HOCKEY ORGANISTS ARE PART OF THE FUN

Organists have been a part of the NHL scene ever since the mid-1920s. With expansion, Norm Kramer in St. Louis made a splash, whipping Blues fans into a frenzy with rah-rah chords on his Wurlitzer.

One of the longest-running popular hockey organists was Gladys Gooding at Madison Square Garden. (Gladys was also the Brooklyn Dodgers' organist at Ebbets Field.) But by far the most acclaimed hockey organist of all was Al Melgard, who began playing for the Chicago Blackhawks in 1927, tickling the fancy of home fans and visitors alike.

Melgard made a practice of hitting the keys during the game, especially after an episode on the ice inspired a tune. For example, if a couple of players started a fight and it broke into a melee, he'd play "Let Me Call You Sweetheart" or "Put Your Arms Around Me Honey."

When a player would be penalized, Melgard would swing into "The Prisoner's Song." One night, a fan tossed a dead squirrel onto the ice and it landed close to Rangers' defenseman Pat Egan. Egan raised his stick like a gun and faked a "bang-bang."

Melgard promptly played "A-Hunting-We-Will-Go." Several referees objected to Melgard playing "Three Blind Mice" when the officials skated out onto the ice. "It was tough enough refereeing without the organist getting the crowd worked up before the game starts," said then-referee King Clancy. But the next time Clancy appeared at a Blackhawks game, Melgard was there playing!

40 | MARCEL PRONOVOST—THE MOST EMBROIDERED MAN IN HOCKEY

Only recently has the National Hockey League created a Department of Player Safety. Unfortunately, it was formed a half-century too late to help defenseman Marcel Pronovost.

A Stanley Cup winner both in Detroit and later Toronto, Pronovost became living proof that hockey is the most dangerous of the team games. And while the NHL never offered an official listing of stitches taken, broken bones suffered, and assorted other injuries, it can be safely stated that nobody was afflicted with more different injuries in more places than the French-Canadian backliner from Lac La Tortue, Quebec.

There are several reasons why Pronovost was so injury-prone. For one thing, he was thoroughly fearless, and for another he played in an era where virtually no players wore helmets and other protective equipment was rather primitive compared with today's armor.

As a result, Marcel's stitch count eventually reached into the hundreds by the time he retired in 1970 after two decades in The Show. As for the broken bones, well, his nose alone was cracked more than a dozen times, and then there was a break of the fourth dorsal vertebrae. Yes, Pronovost even remembered the first time

Hall of Famer Marcel Pronovost, as a Red Wing and Maple Leaf, finished his career as one of the most stitched-up defensemen in the game./*Nam Y. Huh*

his nose lost a battle with an irresistible force: "My eyes were swollen shut for three days."

Undaunted, the defenseman never avoided putting himself in harm's way if it meant helping his club win a hockey game. And since he was what is known as a "rushing defenseman," Pronovost often found himself trying to "split" through the two enemy blue liners on a rush, which was precisely the kind of play that cost Minnesota forward Bill Masterton his life in 1968.

On one such expedition, Marcel was felled by a pincer movement when two opposing defenders simultaneously crushed him. He was catapulted head first over their shoulders before making a three-point landing on his left eyebrow, nose, and cheek.

By the time the wounded Red Wing was taken to the infirmary, his skull was a mess, his nose broken, and twenty-five stitches were needed to close a gash over his left eyebrow. "My cheekbones," said Pronovost, "felt as if they were pulverized." Which was an accurate diagnosis since they were cracked like downed Humpty-Dumpty.

Like so many throwback hockey players, Marcel never betrayed any fear. Actually, the only thing he worried about was missing games due to his mishaps.

"To me," hockey's most injured man once concluded, "accidents are as common as lacing on skates."

That statement is as valid today as it was in 1978 when Joseph Rene Marcel Pronovost was inducted into the Hockey Hall of Fame!

41 | THE MOST TRAVELED STICKHANDLER

The dream of most young boys growing up in the cold winters of Canada is to eventually play on an NHL team. Depending on where they grow up, they may fantasize about the Canadiens, or perhaps imagine themselves skating up and down the ice for the Toronto Maple Leafs, the Detroit Red Wings, or the Boston Bruins.

But for Larry "Morley" Hillman, the dream of playing in the NHL resembled a nightmare as he ended up playing for not only each of the teams listed above, but a host of other NHL, AHL, and WHA clubs during his twenty-plus year career. Twice in his career, Hillman had the dubious distinction of being property of three different professional teams in one day.

Hillman, known to his friends as "Morley," is holder of the dubious honor of being the most traded man in hockey. Hard work and determination helped him crack the NHL in the middle of the 1954-55 season after two and a half years in Junior A with Hamilton and Windsor. Ironically, or perhaps more ominously, Hillman didn't even complete his junior career with one team, as most juniors do, but rather he moved from Windsor (after one year there) to the Hamilton Tiger-Cubs, where he played a year and a half before turning pro with the Detroit Red Wings.

Hillman signed a contract with the Detroit Red Wings and played there for three seasons, but still wasn't getting the ice time he deserved. He was on the roster when the Red Wings were powered to a second Stanley Cup in a row by Ted Lindsay, Gordie Howe, Alex Delvecchio, and goalie Terry Sawchuk. In the summer of 1957, Hillman was drafted from the Red Wings to the Chicago Blackhawks, but never got a chance to pull on the jersey. Just hours before the start of the 1957-58 season, the Boston Bruins picked him up off the Chicago roster.

Hillman appeared in 70 games for the Bruins that year, exceeding by one the number of games he played for Detroit in three seasons. In 1959-60, Hillman was rewarded for his dedication and perseverance with a ticket to the Providence Reds of the AHL. Morley really showed 'em, though. He won the Eddie Shore Award as the league's top defenseman, was selected to the AHL First All-Start team, and to top it off, got a bus ride to Toronto, courtesy of the intra-league draft.

At the age of twenty-three, after over five seasons of being a pro, Hillman was once more packing his bags and moving on to his fourth NHL club. In 1968, after remaining in Toronto for eight seasons (he was constantly shipped between Toronto and AHL affiliate, the Rochester Americans), he was shipped to the New York Rangers. He was content with his time in Toronto, though, as he won four Stanley Cup rings with them.

Amazingly, the same day he was picked up by New York, he was sent out again, this time to the Minnesota North Stars. He was getting close to joining his unprecedented eleventh team in 14 seasons, but after only 12 games with the North Stars, he was again traded again to the Stanley Cup-bound Montreal Canadiens, via the Pittsburgh Penguins in a multi-team deal. Hillman was understandably frustrated; but he was a good sport and saw playing on various teams as a sign that he was a coveted player.

By the end of the 1969 playoffs, Hillman had earned his sixth Stanley Cup ring with Montreal. Unfortunately for Morley, he again changed teams following the season. This time, the four year old Philadelphia Flyers required his services, and responded by posting a career high in goals (5) and points (31).

With the Flyers a full year, it marked only the fifth time in his seventeen-year career that Hillman spent an entire season with one team. Following the 1971 season, Hillman found himself heading west to the Los Angeles Kings in exchange for winger Larry Mickey. Following his brief stay in California, 22 games in total, he was shipped to Buffalo to play for his old nemesis, Punch Imlach. He remained in Buffalo until the 1973 season, when he was obtained by the AHL's Cincinnati Swords.

As the World Hockey Association started gaining in popularity, Morley's rights were shopped around like an unsigned band. Eventually, the Cleveland Crusaders finally secured Hillman from the Chicago Cougars and offered him a contract that included a long-sought after treasure: a no-cut clause.

Cleveland became somewhat of a paradise for Morley, as he was reunited with his younger brother Wayne, and together they became the basis for a fairly strong Cleveland defense, with Boston Bruins defector Gary Cheevers in goal.

Alas, after two seasons in Cleveland, Morley was again shipped out of town, this time into the hands of the Winnipeg Jets of the WHA, which featured the powerful line of Super Swedes, Anders Hedberg, Ulf Nilsson, and the Golden Jet, Bobby Hull. The Jets won the WHA Championship that season, and Hillman retired as a winner.

The saga of Larry "Morley" Hillman is both entertaining and frustrating. He worked for over twenty years to make it, and no matter where he played, coaches and managers whooped and raved about his skill, but then waved good bye.

Despite the dreaded phone calls, Morley never became bitter and always gave 100 percent on the ice with whatever team he was with. But, as Larry would certainly attest, it's impossible to please everybody.

III
Unlikely Heroes

42 | A ONE-EYED REFEREE BECOMES A HALL OF FAMER

The world of athletics is filled with stories about players who overcame physical defects to excel in their respective sports.

In baseball there was Pete Gray, a one-armed center fielder who played the entire 1944 season with the American League's St. Louis Browns. Somehow, Gray managed to bat with his one arm and adroitly field line drives while making adjustments to peg the ball back to the infield and keep runners at bay.

As amazing as Gray's performances were on the field, few could match Bill Chadwick's sweet uses of adversity on the ice.

A New York City native, Chadwick learned to play hockey well enough to make the grade in the Metropolitan League, where he starred for the Jamaica Hawks. His play was so stellar that New York Rangers scouts believed that he eventually could become a successful professional if not a major leaguer on the National Hockey League level. But in March 1935, tragedy struck.

Getting ready for a game at Madison Square Garden between the Met League All-Stars and their Boston counterparts, Chadwick stepped on the ice just as a flying puck—inadvertently shot by a Boston player—struck him in the right eye. The damage was so severe that doctors could not restore his vision, yet when the next season began Chadwick not only returned to the ice but graduated to the Rangers farm team, the New York Rovers of the Eastern League.

"I played center for the Rovers in 1936 and 1937," Chadwick recalled. "And when you played for the Rovers there always was the chance that eventually you might make it to the big club, the Rangers."

Chadwick's future as a scorer looked bright even though his sight was limited to his good left eye. But the good news didn't last very long. While playing for the Rovers, Bill was struck in the left eye—he couldn't be sure whether it was a stick or a puck—and he was in trouble again.

"Blood started trickling into my eye and soon my vision was totally gone," Bill remembered, "only this time I got 'lucky.' My vision eventually returned, but I decided that I had had it as a hockey player."

Instead he became a regular spectator at Rovers' Sunday afternoon games and considered a career on Wall Street. But one day Chadwick showed up at the Garden while a blizzard howled across Manhattan. Suddenly, Tom Lockhart, who then ran the Rovers as well as the Eastern League, discovered that the regular referee was marooned somewhere in the storm. A referee was needed, and Lockhart asked Chadwick to lace up the skates and gave him a whistle.

"Tommy liked my work," said Chadwick, "and eventually I wound up refereeing in the Eastern League. When World War II broke out and they needed an official in the NHL, league president Frank Calder made me one of the league's refs."

At the time it was not widely known that the rookie referee had sight out of only one eye, but soon word leaked out and Chadwick had to work extra hard to prove his worth. "I didn't have much trouble from the players except for a few," Bill said.

A remarkable referee, Hall of Famer Bill Chadwick officiated throughout his career with vision in only one eye./*ASSOCIATED PRESS*

"Maurice Richard of the Montreal Canadiens was one and Ted Lindsay of the Detroit Red Wings was another. Funny, but I never thought that they were on me because of my vision—or lack of it. It was because of their personal makeup; they would have done it to anybody."

Meanwhile, Chadwick was assigned the biggest games as his ability soared during the early 1940s. But he was not immune from official criticism, especially when a club owner believed that his team received a raw deal from Chadwick.

During the 1945 Stanley Cup Final between Detroit and Toronto, the series went to a pulsating seventh—and deciding——game, which was handled by Chadwick.

With the scored tied late in the game, Bill penalized the Red Wings whereupon Babe Pratt of the Maple Leafs scored what proved to be the Cup-winning goal on the ensuing power play. Detroit's owner James Norris was so infuriated that he wanted Chadwick fired but settled, instead, for an annual examination of Bill's good eye to determine whether he still had 20-20 vision.

Chadwick recalled, "Every so often some fan in the balcony would yell down, 'Chadwick, you blind bum.' And I'd chuckle to myself because I knew that they were half-right. One thing I know for sure was that I wasn't a 'homer' anywhere I worked. I would have quit refereeing if I was considered such."

Voted into the Hockey Hall of Fame in 1964, Chadwick finally retired, moving into the broadcasting booth with the likes of Jim Gordon and Marv Albert handling color for Rangers games. He was nicknamed "The Big Whistle" and became one of the most popular hockey broadcasters in New York's history.

One can only imagine what kind of hockey player he would have been had he never lost sight in his right eye. This much is certain; he was a first-rate official and broadcaster as well; not to mention a funny one.

"In the broadcast booth," Bill said, "I even found myself yelling at the referee sometimes, but I was not very proud of it. But I never called a referee a 'blind bat' because I knew I might have been only half-right saying it!"

43 | RED BERENSON—FROM OBSCURITY TO STARDOM IN ONE EASY SIX-GOAL GAME

For the first half of his NHL career, Gordon "Red" Berenson was recognizable for only one thing: he was the only forward in the National Hockey League to wear a helmet.

Otherwise, he appeared to be a flop. First the Montreal Canadiens rejected him after five disappointing years. He was then dealt to the New York Rangers and swiftly was moved on to the St. Louis Blues.

But in the 1968-69 season, Red began flourishing with his third NHL team, and on the night of November 7, 1968, a minor miracle of sorts took place: Red scored not one, not two, not three, not four, not five, but six goals against the Philadelphia Flyers at the Spectrum in Philadelphia.

Nor was the feat accomplished against a flub goalie. Doug Favell was one of the better, young netminders in the NHL, and the Flyers generally played good defense. But Berenson was unstoppable. He scored a goal in the first period and exploded for four in the second and one more in the third and—poof!—just like that, Red emerged as the Babe Ruth of St. Louis hockey; all because of one easy six-goal game.

44 | BILL STEWART–BASEBALL UMPIRE BECOMES BLACKHAWKS COACH; AND WINS A CUP

I t's hard to believe that a renowned National League baseball umpire could suddenly become a hockey coach and almost immediately win a Stanley Cup. But this incredible feat was accomplished in the 1937-38 season.

It was all because multi-millionaire Major Frederic McLaughlin owned the Chicago Blackhawks.

The major had a soft spot for Americans, whether they were players or coaches, and since Bill Stewart was a "nephew" of Uncle Sam, McLaughlin hired Stewart while he was umpiring a ballgame in Philadelphia.

The major sent a wire inviting the Massachusetts-born umpire to both manage and coach the Blackhawks. McLaughlin knew Stewart not only for his superb baseball work but also for his hockey refereeing, which had elevated him to chief arbiter in the NHL.

"The major proposed a one-year contract," said Stewart, "but I was having none of that. When he finally agreed to a two-year contract, I also insisted on an ironclad agreement that I was to be absolute boss."

Stewart was well aware of the major's penchant for interfering with the club. And when McLaughlin wasn't around, there always was the threat of Bill Tobin putting in his two cents' worth. If he could handle the club his way, Stewart believed there would be no problem winning hockey games.

"This was the happiest club I ever saw in professional sport," Stewart has said. "And we had some good talent, too. Players like Gottselig, 'Mush' March, Paul Thompson, Art Wiebe, and Doc Romnes. Lionel Conacher once told me he regarded Romnes as one of the finest centers he ever played with. The biggest reason we won, though, was that we had Earl Siebert on our defense. The guy played about fifty-five minutes of every game."

Stewart's contract may have been "ironclad," but he found the major as omnipresent as ever, and the strong-willed pair feuded and feuded. Usually, Stewart won.

Miraculously, the Blackhawks made the playoffs with an abysmal record of 14-25-9, and yet, somehow, Stewart coached them to the Stanley Cup.

That should have guaranteed a long-term contract for the coach but, guess what? After game 22 of the following season, he was fired.

No problem. Stewart went back to his day job as a baseball umpire and enjoyed a long and successful career.

45 | MALIK ENDS NHL'S LONGEST SHOOTOUT

Early in his career with the New York Rangers, Czech defenseman Marek Malik had earned—fairly or unfairly—the place of (dis)honor for the boobirds at Madison Square Garden. Coming into the November 26, 2005, game against the Washington Capitals, Malik was constantly being hounded for his suspect defensive play, and he had yet to score his first goal of the season.

After a pair of goals from either team, the raucous MSG crowd prepared for overtime. But the game-winning goal was a lot longer in coming.

Rookie sensation Alexander Ovechkin started off the shootout for the visiting team, but his shot was blocked by budding superstar Henrik Lundqvist. Olie Kolzig was equally solid for the Caps, protecting his net from the likes of Martin Straka and Jaromir Jagr.

When one team slipped the puck past the opposing goalie, the other team did the same; and when one goalie came up with a big save, the netminder 200 feet away imitated his performance. Stars were sent out, then second-liners, then offensive defensemen, then fourth-line scrubs. After the twenty-seventh shooter scored for the Caps, perennial fourth-liner Jason Strudwick had the game on his stick. Though Rangers fans were already packing up to go

Marek Malik scored one of the most exciting shootout goals against Washington.
It was in the 15th round./*AP Photo/Julie Jacobson*

home, Strudwick, incredibly, scored, and after Matt Bradley's shot
was saved by Lundqvist, the Rangers had the advantage.

Or did they? As the Blueshirts and the Caps found themselves
in the midst of the NHL's longest shootout, both teams had nearly
exhausted their lineups. Much maligned Marek Malik was one of
the only potential shooters left for the home team, and it's safe to
say he was not known for his clutch goal scoring.

The Czech defenseman appeared none the worse for the wear,
and the look on his face was one of placid confidence as he moved
his 6'6" frame toward the Caps' net. Kolzig's positioning was
impeccable, but Malik had an unexpected trick up his sleeve. The
unflappable Ranger pulled the puck back between his legs and
flipped it over a surprised Kolzig's right shoulder, sealing the win
for the Blueshirts after 15 nail-biting rounds of the shootout.

Malik coolly raised his arms to the crowd in mock-gladiator
fashion as his teammates mobbed him from the bench, and the
Garden faithful erupted in a deafening roar. That a circus-shot like
that had won the game for the home team was incredible; that
Malik was the one who had scored it was even more unbelievable.
Rangers commentator John Davidson put it best that night: "Now
I've seen it all!"

46 | COYOTES PLUCK AMATEUR GOALIE TO SERVE AS BACKUP AFTER ILYA BRYZGALOV FALLS ILL

Tom Fenton was getting his haircut when his cell phone rang.

"This is Brad Treliving, assistant general manager of the Phoenix Coyotes. What are your plans for the night?"

As it turned out, Fenton—a resident of Purchase, New York, and a hockey coach at Manhattanville College—planned on watching that night's Rangers versus Coyotes game from his couch at home. But he ended up watching from the visiting team's bench instead.

"At first, I thought everyone was playing a big joke on me—a couple of my buddies playing a prank," Fenton told MSG Network.

For the Phoenix Coyotes, the situation was no joke. Starting goaltender Ilya Bryzgalov suddenly came down with the flu after the team meal that afternoon, and while backup goalie Jason LaBarbera was prepared to start the game, there would be no one on the bench to replace him in case of an in-game injury. With only several hours to go before the show began on Broadway, the Yotes didn't have enough time to call up a goalie from its affiliate in San Antonio. Hockey ops considered signing goaltending coach and former NHLer Sean Burke for the game, but he would have to pass through the 24-hour waiver period.

Tom Fenton (seated, right, on the bench) was a goalie who never expected to
wear a Phoenix uniform. He looks on at the NHL action./*AP Photo/*
Frank Franklin II

Enter American International College graduate Tom Fenton.
The Coyotes organization had scoured the area for a local amateur
goalie, making several phone calls and hearing no voices on
the other end. When Treliving put the call through to Fenton, it
seemed like another dead-end—but Fenton called back immediately, and was given the opportunity of a lifetime.

The twenty-six-year-old Sarnia, Ontario, native hadn't played
a game of organized hockey since his college days in Springfield,
Massachusetts. And after signing an emergency contract with
the Phoenix Coyotes, he was about to suit up for his first—and
only—NHL game.

"I was a little shaky at first," Fenton admitted to MSG.

Fenton took warmups with his new team, adorned in NHL
goalie equipment and his very own Phoenix Coyotes jersey (which
he got to keep afterward). His teammates went easy on him before
the game, but Fenton had a sudden vision of being forced into the

game by a freak LaBarbera injury and having Rangers' winger Marian Gaborik bearing down on him menacingly with the puck.

Luckily, Fenton started and finished the game on the bench, soaking in the NHL action from the best seat in the house with wide-eyed awe. Coyotes captain Shane Doan joked to FSN Arizona that he and his teammates were trying to get the newbie onto the scoresheet, but Fenton was fine just where he was.

Phoenix broadcaster Todd Walsh reported: "As long as I live, I will never forget the look on Fenton's face when he was told to get out of the line of players heading to the locker room and head to the interview area just off the ice behind the visiting goal at the 'World's Most Famous Arena.'"

Needless to say, Tom Fenton will never forget that night either.

47 | HOW A BUSHER WON THE LONGEST PLAYOFF GAME

Under ordinary circumstances you would think that the longest game in Stanley Cup history was decided by a superstar's goal.

But when a match extends into 6 extra periods, just about anything can happen.

Certainly, on the night of March 24, 1936, just about everything *did* happen.

One of the most incredible circumstances involved the goalie for the Montreal Maroons against Detroit.

Montreal's goalie just happened to be Lorne Chabot, who tended goal for the Toronto Maple Leafs on April 3-4, 1933, in what previously had been the longest overtime game in history.

Another similarity came under the heading of "Heroes."

In the first longest game, a third-stringer, Ken Doraty, ended the marathon.

And when that record was broken three years later, the winning goal was tallied by a player who barley was good enough to make a dent in the Detroit roster.

His name was Modere Bruneteau, known to his teammates as "Mud."

Like Doraty three years earlier, Bruneteau was thrust into the breach because fatigue had afflicted his more talented teammates.

As for the record-breaking game itself, there was good reason to expect a marathon simply because the Maroons and Red Wings had almost identical records. Led by Hooley Smith, Baldy Northcott, and Jimmy Ward, the Maroons presented one of the most formidable attacks in the league. The Red Wings' first line of Marty Barry, Herbie Lewis, and Larry Aurie had an impressive season, with Barry winning the scoring title in the American Division.

Despite the notable scorers on both teams, three periods of play elapsed without either club scoring a goal. This meant sudden-death overtime; the first team to score would win the game.

Although the Montreal Forum crowd was excited about the prospect of sudden death, there was some reason to suspect this might be an exceptionally long night. For one thing, the teams were getting excellent goaltending from Normie Smith in the Red Wing cage and Chabot of the Maroons. For another, there was precedent for a marathon match. On April 4, 1933, the Toronto Maple Leafs and Boston Bruins played past 1 a.m. in what had been the longest NHL game on record.

By the time the Maroons and Red Wings had played through the second overtime without a goal, the crowd began to get restless. The players, of course, were laboring on badly chopped ice that didn't have the benefit of modern resurfacing machines in vogue today. Nevertheless, they plodded on past midnight with no end in sight.

When the sixth period began, a cascade of cheers went up from the previously numbed crowd. Perhaps they hoped to inspire the Maroons to a spirited rush and a score, but this didn't happen. Neither team scored, and the teams moved into the seventh period as a handful of fans streamed to the exits.

Despite the hour, the majority of spectators remained in their seats. By now the monumental contest became an obsession with both players and fans, and everyone seemed determined to see it through to a conclusion, no matter what happened. Nothing very much happened in the seventh period, but the eighth period (or fifth sudden death period) loomed as the decisive one.

Near the end of the period, Marty Barry, the Red Wings' accomplished center, was approaching collapse. With the energy he had at his command, Barry sent a pass to Herbie Lewis that catapulted his wing into the clear for a play on goal. He moved into striking distance and released a hard shot that obviously beat goalie Lorne Chabot. As Lewis prepared to raise his stick in the traditional victory salute, he heard the puck clang off the goal post. It rebounded harmlessly to the corner, where Hooley Smith retrieved it and began a counterattack with as much danger as Lewis' play.

Smith was accompanied on the rush by Baldy Northcott. There was a choice—either Smith could make the play himself, using Northcott as a decoy, or he could try the pass. At first Smith cut sharply toward the net, giving the impression he would go it alone. But, at this precise moment, he skimmed the puck to Northcott, who shot hard at the Red Wing net. However, Normie Smith anticipated the play, caught the puck on his pad, and steered it to teammate Doug Young, who reversed the field.

Now, it appeared that each team was bent on wild kamikaze attacks in the hopes of bringing the game to a sudden end. Young raced along the boards until he reached Maroon territory. Then he fired wildly, but the puck suddenly hit Maroon defenseman Lionel Conacher's skate and changed direction, sliding straight for an empty side of the net. It appeared to be equidistant between Young and the goalie Chabot. The Red Wing skater lunged for it, but before he could get his stick on the rubber, Chabot smothered it with his glove. Shortly thereafter the period ended, and the teams had completed 8 scoreless periods of play.

Four minutes and 46 seconds after the ninth period began, the teams had broken the longest-game record set by Toronto and Boston, and still there was no end in sight. It was past 2 a.m., and many of the spectators were fighting to keep their eyes open, not wanting to miss the decisive goal if it ever was scored.

By this time, the veterans of both teams were fatigued beyond recovery. It was essential to employ the players with the most stamina and, naturally, those with even a smidgen of energy remaining were the inexperienced younger skaters. One of them was Modere (Mud) Bruneteau, a native of St. Boniface, Manitoba, who had just one season ago played for the Wings' minor league team, the Detroit Olympics. He was the youngest man in the longest game, Jack Adams believed, with the strongest legs. Adams was the Detroit coach and he remembered, before he died in 1968: "The game settled into an endurance test, hour after hour. One o'clock came, and then 2 a.m., and by now the ice was a chopped brutal mess. At 2:25, I looked along our bench for the strongest legs and I scrambled the lines to send out Syd Howe, Hec Kilrea, and Bruneteau."

As a rookie on a loaded first-place club, Bruneteau saw very little action during the season and scored only two goals while achieving no assists for a grand total of two points. But he was young, and at the 12-minute mark of the ninth period, Mud Bruneteau was in a lot better shape than most of his teammates or opponents.

Adams' instructions were typically explicit. "Boys, let's get some sleep. It's now or never!"

Bruneteau surrounded the puck in the Detroit zone and passed it to Kilrea. They challenged the Montreal defense, Kilrea faking a return pass, then sliding it across the blueline. Bruneteau cut behind the defense and retrieved the puck. "Thank God," he says, "Chabot fell down as I drove it in the net. It was the funniest thing. The puck just stuck there in the twine and didn't fall on the ice."

There was a dispute when the goal judge neglected to flash his red light, but referee Nels Stewart arbitrated. "You bloody right it's a goal!" Stewart announced, and put up his hand as a signal. After 116 minutes and 30 seconds of overtime, the Red Wings had defeated the Maroons, 1-0.

There was a wild, capering anticlimax. Bruneteau's sweater was removed, not delicately, by his relieved associates. One fan thrust a $20 bill on Bruneteau as he left the ice. Other exuberants reached for their wallets. "There I was with my stick under one arm and my gloves under another," he said, laughing. "I grabbed money in every direction!"

When he reached the Detroit dressing room, Bruneteau tossed a bundle of bills on a rubbing table. "Count it," he told Honey Walker, the trainer, "and split it for the gang." The windfall was gratifying for players in a depression year: $22 for each member of the Wings, including Adams, Walker, and the stickboy.

Mud Bruneteau's shot went into the net at 16:30 of the sixth overtime, or 2:25 a.m. Eastern Standard Time. Normie Smith, who was playing in his first Stanley Cup game, was limp when it was over. He had stopped 90 shots in all. "We were all pretty much all in it," Smith recalled years later, "but very happy."

Meanwhile, Bruneteau sat on his bed in Montreal's genteel Windsor Hotel near 5 a.m. on March 25, 1936, still unwinding from a Stanley Cup playoff that he had won for Detroit Red Wings' less than three hours before. He was about to undress after a beer celebration when there came a knock on the door. He sat very still, not caring to be disturbed. The knocker persisted. Finally, Bruneteau let his visitor in, and was somewhat startled to recognize the Montreal Goal-keeper he had beaten to end the weary marathon. Lorne Chabot, dark eyes staring under a thicket of black brows, had come to call. "Sorry to bother you, kid," Chabot said, "but you forgot something when you left the rink." Then he handed Bruneteau a puck, "Maybe you'd like to have this souvenir of the goal you scored."

48 | THE TOTALLY IMPROBABLE DEVILS 1988 PLAYOFF RUN

Starting in 1982 and for the next five years of the Devils' existence, New Jersey's big-league hockey franchise became the laughing stock of the NHL. Season after season, coaches came and went without any satisfaction for the owner, Dr. John McMullen.

Finally, during the 1987-88 campaign—which had the earmarks of another non-playoff disaster—McMullen boldly hired Lou Lamoriello, who had gained renown for running a successful Providence College athletic program. After reviewing his team for about a month before Christmas 1987, Lamoriello fired coach Doug Carpenter, replacing him with Jim Schoenfeld.

The new bench boss added a spark, and the arrival of Canadian Olympic goalie Sean Burke after the Winter Games in Calgary provided another boost along with sharpshooter John MacLean. Still, a playoff berth was too far distant to contemplate, and besides, to reach the post-season, New Jersey would have to catch and pass a good Rangers club.

But as the schedule reached the homestretch, something special happened to the Garden Staters—they went on a winning rampage. Relentlessly, they narrowed the gap until, on the final night of the regular season, April 3, 1988, it was mathematically

From the 1988 Canadian Olympic team, Sean Burke went on to become the Devils' surprise playoff star that Spring./*ASSOCIATED PRESS*

possible for the Devils to do what they never had done before—make the playoffs.

To do so, it meant winning a game at Chicago Stadium; a tie would not do. Meanwhile, the Rangers would be playing the Quebec Nordiques at Madison Square Garden. If the Rangers won—which they did 3-0 earlier in the evening—Schoenfeld's skaters still could squeeze in with a victory; a tie would not do the trick.

As luck would have it, the Devils came from behind midway in the third period to tie the game 3-3, sending it into overtime. Burke was in goal for New Jersey.

49 | THE MYSTERY NHL CAMEO APPEARANCE OF LARRY KWONG

Following their 1940 Stanley Cup championship, the New York Rangers relied heavily on their Madison Square Garden-based farm team, the New York Rovers, for future talent.

And without fail, the Eastern League club delivered talent, season by season. In fact, during the 1945-46 campaign, the Rovers delivered an entire forward unit—Cal Gardner, Rene Trudell, and Church Russell—to the big club. Since it was shortly after World War II—and everyone remembered the atomic bomb dropped on Hiroshima, Japan—the trio was nicknamed The Atomic Line.

Shortly thereafter, the Rovers produced another productive unit comprised of Nick (Bashful-Nick-Ready-To-Click) Mickoski, Ian (Mickey) MacIntosh, and Larry (King) Kwong. Occasionally Hub Anslow would replace Mickoski on the line.

Mickoski was regarded as the best of the threesome and was promoted in 1947. Nick enjoyed a National Hockey League career for more than a decade and was one of the most popular Rangers until his trade to Chicago on Thanksgiving Eve 1954. MacIntosh had a four-game "cup of coffee" with the Blueshirts and was deemed a good minor leaguer who couldn't quite cut it on Broadway.

And then there was Kwong, who cut it big; but in Chinatown more than the NHL. A native of Vernon, British Columbia, Kwong was descended from a Chinese family that emigrated to Canada in the late 1880s. Like most Canadian lads, Larry learned his hockey on frozen ponds and proved to be more adept at it than most of the neighboring kids and in time made his way up the hockey ladder playing for the local Vernon Hydrophones and then the Trail Smoke Eaters, a legendary team in western Canada.

After a stint in the Canadian Army during World War II, Kwong showed up at the Rangers training camp in Winnipeg where he impressed the Blueshirts scouts to a point where he was offered a minor league pact with the Rovers.

In those halcyon post-war days, the Rovers were almost as popular in Gotham as the Rangers and crowds of more than twelve thousand to fifteen thousand were not uncommon. In fact, on one Sunday, the Rovers actually drew more fans than the parent Rangers.

It was in that atmosphere that Larry became a Rovers star. Although he checked in at 5-6, 145 pounds, Kwong never was intimidated by the bigger players on the opposition. Plus, he had a very special cheering section. As the first player of Chinese descent to appear in a New York hockey uniform, Larry became the darling of Chinatown. As David Davis wrote in *The New York Times*, "Before one Rovers game, Shavey Lee, the unofficial mayor of Chinatown, and two showgirls from the China Doll night club, honored a blushing Kwong at center ice. He was called King Kwong and the China Clipper."

Like many others who regularly attended Rovers games, I wondered when Larry would get his Rangers audition as did Gardner, Russell, and Trudell. I was impressed during virtually every game with Kwong's speed, smarts, and teamsmanship.

In a way he reminded me of Hall of Famer Yvon Cournoyer, the Montreal Canadiens forward nicknamed "Roadrunner."

Larry's "break"—if it could be called that—finally came during a thrilling 1947-48 season. For five straight seasons, beginning with America's entry into World War II, the Rangers had missed the playoffs and now, at last, it appeared that they would snare the fourth and final playoff berth.

In the waning weeks of the season, as the Blueshirts fought off the Canadiens for the last playoff berth, a spate of injuries decimated New York's roster and on March 13, 1948, general manager and coach Frank Boucher promoted Kwong to the Rangers along with his Rovers teammate Ron Rowe. Not surprisingly, Kwong was filled with pride and the anticipation of proving that he was big-league calibre.

"That's what I wanted to be since I was a kid in Vernon," Kwong recalled. "To be in the NHL."

Kwong, who turned ninety-years-old in 2013, still shakes his head in disbelief at what ensued in that memorable game against such Hall of Famers as Maurice (Rocket) Richard and Doug Harvey.

Coach Boucher wasted no time sending Rowe out against the Habs but Kwong remained on the bench impatiently awaiting the nod from his boss. He waited through the first period and the second, but still no call from Boucher. Now the score was 2-2 late in the third period and, finally, Kwong was given the green light and for one minute he was living his dream—in The Show.

But when the minute was up, Larry was again riding the pines until the game ended.

No problem; the Rangers were playing the next night at Madison Square Garden and Kwong looked forward to making his Manhattan debut but was stunned to learn that he was not dressing for the game. Rovers teammates Rowe and Herb Foster were going to be skating for the Blueshirts.

Did King Kwong disgrace himself in his NHL premiere? Hardly. The one-minute shift was without incident and that was it.

Was prejudice involved? Very doubtful, since Boucher was a fair-minded fellow not given to ethnic bias of any kind.

Therein lies the mystery; why didn't Larry get another chance? The best answer came from Montreal Hall of Fame left wing Dickie Moore who explained: "It all depended on management and the coach and what type of player they were looking for." My guess is that Boucher considered King Kwong—right or wrong—too small to compete. Meanwhile, the Rangers sneaked into fourth place and the final playoff berth and were eliminated in the first round by the Detroit Red Wings.

Conceivably, Larry might have made the varsity next season had he hung around New York—which he admittedly loved— for one more year. But he was in his prime and high-class outfits such as Quebec Senior Hockey League were paying big money to players of Larry's ability. One such team was the Valleyfield (Quebec) Braves, coached by Toe Blake, who later would lead Montreal to five consecutive Stanley Cups. Not surprisingly, Kwong was among the leading scorers on one of Canada's top teams. Meanwhile, the Kwong-less Rangers missed the playoffs.

But he never got a nod from another NHL team and eventually retired. Looking backward, Kwong admitted that he never questioned Boucher's decision to employ him for only one minute in one NHL game; an incredible mistake in retrospect.

"In those days," Kwong concluded, "a player didn't question management. Boucher had his team and that was that."

And in one precious minute, that *was* that for King Kwong's NHL career.

Or, as a headline in the *New York World-Telegram* newspaper so aptly put it: *WHAT'S KWONG WITH THE RANGERS?*

50 | THERE IS A TAVERN–AND A GOALIE–IN THE TOWN (Alfie Moore)

This couldn't happen in contemporary hockey because every National Hockey League club has a second (backup) goalie.

But in April 1938 it was a different story; an incredible one when you come to think of it.

A minor league goaltender who happened to be quaffing a beer in a Toronto tavern wound up being the unlikely hero who helped bring a Stanley Cup to Chicago.

Even more unreal—at least according to normal big-league hockey standards—was the fact that the Blackhawks of that spring just happened to finish the regular season 11 wins *under* the .500 mark. (14-25-9).

How could this happen?

To begin with, the Windy City sextet qualified for the postseason under a weird NHL system that enabled three out of the four teams in the then-American Division to enter the playoffs. And once on the Playoff Highway, the Hawks could not be stopped.

First they upset the Montreal Canadiens, two games to one in a best-of-three series and then repeated the feat against the favored New York Americans to reach the Cup Final with the Toronto Maple Leafs as the foe.

Mathematically, it appeared to be an open-netter for the Leafs. They led the Canadian Division with a formidable 24-15-9 record and opened the best-of-five series at their home Maple Leaf Gardens.

If Chicagoans had any hope for an upset, it was thanks to the superlative goaltending of Minnesota-born Mike Karakas, but on the eve of the Cup round it was discovered that Iron Mike was *hors de combat*. A broken toe sustained while eliminating the Americans made it impossible for the netminder to lace on his skates. Since NHL teams only carried one puck-stopper in those early NHL days, the Blackhawks suddenly found themselves in deep trouble.

What to do? Traditionally, clubs which were out of the playoffs were known to "loan" goalies to teams in dire need. And one just happened to be available—Toronto native Davey Kerr, who played for the New York Rangers. The trick would be getting an okay from Maple Leafs boss Conn Smythe, who was regarded as the Royal Highness of Hockey, in some ways more powerful that NHL president Frank Calder.

Approached by the Blackhawks' high command for permission to "borrow" Kerr for the opening game, Smythe shot back, something akin to no, no, a thousand times no!

That said, Chicago's general staff huddled and when the strategy session was over, it was agreed that a Toronto-wide search would be conducted by every Blackhawks employee then in Canada's Queen City. And since it generally was accepted that off-duty goalies were not averse to quaff a pint or two, several of the netminder-searchers headed for popular Toronto taverns.

It was a crap-shoot to be sure but, realistically, it was the only hope since, the opening faceoff was just hours away. Someone in the Chicago entourage mentioned that another goaltender who happened to be a Toronto resident *was* available. His name was

Alfie Moore and he spent most of his time in the minors. What's more, the "scouts" knew about Alfie's favorite tavern and, sure enough, he was found and signed to a Blackhawks contract.

That night Moore laced on the pads for the vital first game—vital because the Final round in those days was best-of-five and the opener often set the tone for the series—backed by a team determined to get even with Conn Smythe.

At first, Moore faltered, allowing a goal by Leafs sharpshooter Gordie Drillon, but the visitors counterattacked. Successive goals by Johnny Gottselig, Paul Thompson, and Gottselig again put Chicago ahead, 3-1 in the third period while Moore was flawless in goal.

The jubilant Windy City skaters embraced the unlikeliest of heroes and coach Bill Stewart announced that Alfie would start Game Two, also at Maple Leaf Gardens. But Smythe protested that Moore was ineligible for a second game in goal and NHL president Frank Calder ruled in Toronto's favor, demanding that Chicago insert Paul Goodman, their minor league puck-stopper who had never played an NHL game before.

Goodman was shelled 5-1, but by the time the teams moved on to Chicago Stadium for Games Three and Four, Mike Karakas had recovered from his injury. With the spirit of Alfie Moore behind him, Karakas won two straight from the Leafs, 2-1 and 4-1 for the Blackhawks' second Stanley Cup.

Many will debate what the final result would have been had Smythe granted permission to use Davey Kerr, but the bottom line is that Alfie Moore put down his glass of beer and came to the rescue. Hence, Alfie's name is on The Stanley Cup.

P.S. Kerr eventually made the Cup list two years later when his Rangers beat Smythe's Leafs in six games!

51 | MIRACLE MYLES

Among the graduates of the NHL, some of whom have traveled from the ice to the Canadian Parliament, New York State Supreme Court Judge Myles J. Lane ranked as one of the most distinguished. He began wearing the black robes on January 1, 1969. Before that, he was a member of the New York State Commission of Investigation, a team of top-level gangbusters which he joined after working as a U.S. attorney.

Lane was also the first American ever to play on a Stanley Cup team, the Boston Bruins of 1929. Hockey helped Lane become a lawyer. He worked his way through law school by playing the game—first for the Rangers, then for the Bruins—and by managing the Boston Cubs, a Bruins farm team.

Lane was a competent player, if not a star. And as one of the first Americans in the big leagues, he had tremendous curiosity value at the box office. This was not always to his advantage though.

In a locker room interview after his first Rangers game, a sportswriter misquoted Lane as saying that "this game is a cinch compared to college hockey." When the Rangers arrived in Montreal the following Saturday night, the newspapers were exhorting the populace to come out and see the wise guy.

The arena was packed. The Montreal Maroons were out to get the college boy who had scoffed at the Canadian professionals.

Lane's first rush down the ice ended with a bone-crushing bodycheck and a charging penalty for his overanxious opponent. His next rush ended the same way and so did the third.

Emotions were running high, and the game grew rougher. Lane escaped unhurt, but by the time the game was over, there were two major casualties. Taffy Abel needed twelve stitches in his foot, and the great Ching Johnson broke his leg, an injury from which he never fully recovered.

Lane thought of Johnson as a big brother and mentor, but as for the greatest player he ever saw, Lane gives the award to Eddie Shore, then of the Bruins. He was not alone in his admiration. When Lane was with the Rangers, the Blueshirts tried to set up a deal that would have involved trading Eddie Shore for Myles Lane. The Boston reply was quick and to the point: "You're so many Myles from Shore, you need a life preserver!"

52 | HOW ONE OF HOCKEY'S GREATEST STARS WAS DISCOVERED ON THE FOOTBALL FIELD

Conn Smythe was watching a football game between McMaster University and a Toronto intermediate team one afternoon with his wife. Smythe's attention was arrested by a large McMaster halfback, who appeared to be manipulating the game with an assortment of runs, catches, and kicks. After the game, Smythe inquired whether the player knew how to play hockey. He was told that Sylvanius Apps was, indeed, an accomplished hockey player, not to mention the best pole vaulter in Canada.

Apps, however, was not persuaded that he should pursue a hockey career with the pros. He wanted to compete in the 1936 Olympics and also considered other careers when the Olympics were over. But he agreed to meet with Smythe when the game ended. Once Apps returned, he couldn't refuse Smythe's offer. He signed with the Maple Leafs and became one of Canada's most respected hockey players. He won the Calder Trophy as Rookie of the Year in his first season and, in time, became captain and leader of the Leafs during their golden era in the late 1940s.

Apps was described as the Bobby Orr of his day by hockey experts. Long and lean, Syl had developed a graceful skating style which would later inspire Montreal author Vincent D. Lunny to call him "a Rembrandt on the ice, a Nijinsky at the goalmouth."

Apps also had all of Canada behind him after returning from the eleventh Olympiad in Berlin, Germany, where before 100,000 spectators including Adolf Hitler, he vaulted to a sixth place tie for Canada. Even Jack Adams, the Detroit Red Wings' manager who always was grudging in his praise of Toronto players, had to admit: "He's better than Howie Morenz was at the same age," when Apps emerged as an NHL star as a twenty-one-year-old rookie.

While he was earning his place among hockey greats, Syl also managed to take his first turn in the political arena. He was nominated as the conservative candidate for the federal election in North Brant. He was defeated in the election, however, and once again concentrated on hockey full time. In 1948, Apps led the Leafs to first place and the Stanley Cup, then retired from pro hockey and went on to become a member of the Ontario Legislature for Kingston and a member of the cabinet.

53 | JOE MILLER—A JOKE BOOK AND A GOALIE

Goalie Joe Miller emerged as something of a joke around NHL circles in the late twenties, despite some rather competent goaltending. Miller broke into the majors with the New York Americans in 1927-28.

At the time, the Amerks were the lowest-scoring team in the league, which didn't help Joe very much, although he had the ninth-worst GAA (goals against average) in the ten-team league. Madison Square Garden fans dubbed him "Red Light" Miller, and he was kidded throughout the game.

But Joe's moment of glory was soon to come. During the 1928 Stanley Cup playoffs between the Montreal Maroons and the New York Rangers, regular New York goalie Lorne Chabot was seriously injured in the second game of the series.

Manager Lester Patrick substituted for Chabot during the game in which his regular goaltender was hurt and led the Rangers to victory. But Lester had no intentions of playing after that game, and Chabot was still shelved. It was then that Miller stepped in—with the permission of the Maroons—and took the net for the Rangers for the rest of the series.

In Miller's first game as a Ranger—the series was tied one apiece in the best-of-five playoff—the Maroons won, 2-0, although Joe played very well. But in the fourth game, the Rangers managed a goal and Miller blanked the Maroons, tying the finals at two games each.

Miller was sensational again in the finale, allowing only one Montreal score. The Rangers had scored twice and captured their first Stanley Cup with a 2-1 triumph and a 3-2 victory in games. "Joe Miller," wrote Lou Marsch in *The Toronto Star*, "the substitute goalie, was the hero."

Despite his heroics, Miller found himself dealt to Pittsburgh in 1929. He played two full seasons with the Pirates and then was dealt to the Philadelphia Quakers, where he ended his major league career in 1930-31. Ironically, Joe Miller's only NHL playoff adventure took place with the Rangers, the team that didn't even own him—and that's no joke!

54 | THE MOST TOTALLY IMPROBABLE TWO-GOALIE ROTATION

When the New York (Brooklyn) Americans folded in 1942, their starting goalie, Chuck Rayner, entered the armed forces. When Rayner was discharged at war's end, the Americans were no longer in existence, so his contract was picked up by the New York Rangers, who also had a first-rate goalie in James (Sugar Jim) Henry, who happened to be a good friend of Rayner and partner in a motel with him.

Rangers manager Lester Patrick decided to retain both goalies, and his coach, Frank Boucher, even went so far as to alternate them during games. "I would change goalies every five minutes," said Boucher. "At one point, we only had one pair of gloves for the two goalies, so every time they passed each other during a change they'd transfer gloves—which looked kind of funny at the time."

"It was great at first," recalled Rayner. "Jim Henry and I both enjoyed it. We didn't switch off games, we switched off shifts. About every third or fourth line change, we would change. It was alright in the beginning, but it became a problem later. I would be in goal and just get warmed up when there would be a line change and I would come off. Then Sugar Jim got in there, and by the time he'd warmed up, out he'd come."

55 | HOW THE SKINNIEST GUY BECAME A TOP SCORER

Camille Henry was not nicknamed The Eel for nothing. The fact that he survived fifteen-plus years in the NHL was considered miraculous since he was so thin and apparently fragile.

Even when he showed up at Rangers training camp in September 1953, he was not expected to make the big club. Then, one of those miracles of fate took place, and The Eel became a big fish on Broadway.

How could this have happened?

"Max Bentley got sick a few hours before game time, and Mr. Boucher called me up and told me I was going to play instead. By the end of the preseason schedule, I had more points than any other center on the team," Henry remembered.

"Mr. Boucher called me when we were breaking camp—I thought he was going to tell me he was sending me down to the minor league team—and he said to me 'Cammy, I think you can make the National Hockey League. I have my twenty players right now, but I would like to carry you with the team because I think you can learn a lot just from watching.'

"The season started in Detroit, and I didn't dress. In the second period, Dean Prentice dislocated his shoulder, giving me my chance. The next night we were in Chicago, and Boucher told me to dress. We won 5-2; I scored a goal and got an assist."

Cammy never looked back. He finished the year with 24 goals and 39 points, and the Calder Trophy as the league's top rookie, beating Jean Beliveau. Before Camille became a great player, he was lucky enough to be surrounded by a few.

"Max Bentley was the biggest help I ever had in hockey for one simple reason—he talked hockey with me non-stop. If I wanted to stay up all night talking about how to play certain guys and what to do in certain types of situations, Max would stay up with me. When we went on road trips and had those long train rides, he used to have to kick me out of his room at five in the morning, that's all we would do. Talk hockey.

"He was also a very exciting player to watch. I remember one night we were in Detroit, and Max told me he was going to score a goal against them, and this was when they had guys like Howe, Lindsay, Delvecchio, Red Kelly, and Sawchuk in nets. So I told him if he was going to score one, I was going to score one, too.

"In the second period we had a power play, and Max was on the ice. He took the puck on his stick and skated all the way down the ice through Howe, Lindsay, Kelly, Bob Goldham and then put a move on Sawchuk and scored the goal. He skated over to the bench and winked. I said, 'Don't forget about me' and he said 'Don't worry, you'll score.'

"We were out on the ice about a minute later when Max got the puck again. He started a mad dash toward the Detroit goal, right through their defense, just like the first time. He got right in front of Sawchuk, pulled him out and had him cold turkey, but instead of shooting he passed the puck over to where I had come down on the left side. There was no way in the world I could have missed, so I out the puck in the net just that easy. That's what kind of guy Max Bentley was."

PS: Ever since his rookie year, Henry was given a program for adding weight to his streamline fuselage. After one season in New York, the Rangers' high command urged him to return to his native Quebec City and drink two chocolate malt drinks every day until training camp began.

The hope was that a few pounds—maybe a dozen—would be added to his 135-pound frame.

Cammy did what he was told and, low and behold, when he returned to camp in September, he still weighed 135 pounds!

After all, they didn't call him The Eel for nothing.

56 | PUNCH IMLACH'S IMPROBABLE PLAYOFF CRUSADE

To say that New York Rangers coach Phillipe Henri (Phiery Phil) Watson and his Toronto Maple Leafs counterpart George (Punch) Imlach didn't like each other would be the understatement of the half-century.

This rivalry reached a crescendo during the 1958-59 season when Watson's Blueshirts were riding high while Imlach struggled to turn a makeshift Leafs lineup into a playoff contender.

Under Watson, the Rangers had made the playoffs each season since he took command of the club in October 1955. Fortified with future Hall of Famers such as Andy Bathgate, Bill Gadsby, Lorne (Gump) Worsley, and Harry Howell, the New Yorkers actually appeared good to challenge the Stanley Cup champion Montreal Canadiens, which already had won three straight titles.

Imlach, who had replaced Billy Reay after the Leafs' twentieth game in the fall of 1958, inherited a team blended with old-timers such as Allan Stanley and Tim Horton on defense with ancient Johnny Bower in goal as well as a promising crop of youngsters led by gifted Frank Mahovlich.

It was generally acknowledged that Imlach would require at least two years to turn Toronto into a formidable force. However, Punch was not the patient type, and somehow he sensed that his outfit could beat the odds and squeeze into the fourth and final playoff berth.

To do so, several elements had to break in the Leafs favor and, as luck would have it, they all involved the Rangers in general and Watson in particular.

While the Rangers were riding high, Watson nevertheless became a tormentor of his troops. On one occasion, after an especially tough game against the Canadiens at Madison Square Garden, he forced his player to endure a mean-spirited one-hour drill on the ice. When it was over, Rangers power play specialist Camille Henry confessed to a reporter that "This [drill] could hurt us in the homestretch."

That didn't seem possible at the time, but other developments intruded including a classic one-on-one fight between New York defenseman Lou (Leapin' Louie) Fontinato and Detroit's Hall of Fame right wing Gordie Howe at The Garden.

For a couple of seasons, Fontinato was regarded as the unofficial heavyweight champion of the league; that is, until he was pulverized by Howe's fists. As a result not only was Leapin' Louie demoralized, so was the entire Rangers team.

Sensing that something unpredictably good might happen to his team, Imlach began chirping to the media that he believed his Maple Leafs could catch the Rangers and squeeze into the fourth and final playoff berth. Most observers treated Punch's optimism as mere press fodder, but the comments touched a nerve with Watson, who seemed to overreact. And the more Phiery Phil exploded over the Punch-talk, Imlach machine-gunned more digs in the direction of New York.

Meawhile the gap between the Leafs and Rangers began to narrow, and with two weeks remaining in the schedule, seven points separated fifth place Toronto from fourth place New York.

By any standards that still was a substantial margin, but more misfortune afflicted the Rangers. Facing the Leafs in New York, the Rangers appeared to have at least a tie wrapped up and that would keep the seven-point margin intact. But late in the third period, Toronto center Bob Pulford skated to center ice and then readied for a line change.

Before turning toward the bench, Pulford tossed an innocent wrist shot toward Rangers goalie Lorne (Gump) Worsley. What should have been a simple play turned into a disaster; Worsley blew the shot and Toronto won the game.

By now Imlach was believing his promise to make the playoffs while Watson was beside himself with angst, and for good reason. One by one, the Rangers continued to lose games while the Maple Leafs kept putting up Ws.

By the final night of the season, Watson's skaters still could have clinched fourth by beating the Canadiens at The Garden. The Leafs, however, were in Detroit facing the Red Wings and legendary goalie Terry Sawchuk. The only way that Imlach could exit smiling was by winning while the Rangers lost.

The night started well for Watson. Harry Howell scored for the Blueshirts in the first period and the Garden crowd went wild. But that was it for the Rangers; Montreal answered with three straight goals and won the game, 3-1.

In The Motor City, Imlach had to wait since the game there started an hour later than the Garden tilt. But once it began, a see-saw effect took place. First the Red Wings went ahead, then the Leafs came back, and so it went into the third period, when Larry Regan of the Leafs put his club ahead to stay.

Toronto was in; New York was out.

Imlach would go on to win Stanley Cups with his Leafs in 1962, 1963, 1964, and 1967.

Watson was fired as Rangers coach after 15 games in the 1959-60. He later coached the Bruins in 1961-62—disastrously—and was fired after 14 games the following season. Phiery Phil never coached again in the NHL. Imlach went on to a long career as both general manager and coach in Toronto and later with the Buffalo Sabres.

Guess Punch won that argument!

57

HOW MICKEY MOUSE BECAME A RALLYING CRY FOR THE DEVILS FRANCHISE

Turning fiction into fact isn't easy when you're dealing with a Walt Disney character such as Mickey Mouse.

But the cartoon character came to life during the 1983-84 season, the New Jersey Devils' second in the National Hockey League. And who did the New Jersey sextet have to thank for bringing the little rodent onto the Devils bandwagon?

Incredibly it was none other than Wayne Gretzky, the most productive big-leaguer of all-time.

The saga unfolded on the night of November 19, 1983, in Edmonton after The Great One's Oilers demolished New Jersey 13-4. It represented the largest score ever run up against the franchise.

And the swarming was not over yet.

Reporters descended on the Oilers' dressing room for comments, especially from Gretzky, who had eight points on three goals and five assists.

Prodded with leading questions from the newsmen, the still naïve Gretzky was lured into a denunciation that he would have avoided, had he had the luxury of replay.

"It got to a point where it wasn't even funny," said Gretzky. "How long has it been for them? Three years? Five? Seven?

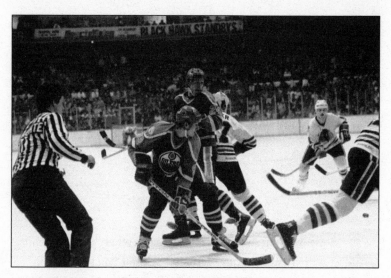

Wayne Gretzky (left) made the mistake of calling the New Jersey Devils, "A Mickey Mouse Outfit." He went on to regret that slur. *AP Photo/Fred Jewel*

Probably closer to nine. Well, it's time they got their act together. They're ruining the whole league. They had better stop running a Mickey Mouse organization and put somebody on the ice."

The game took place on a Saturday night in Edmonton, and by Monday the headlines were blaring all over the country. "GRETZKY TAKES SLAP AT DEVILS ORGANIZATION" barked the headline in *USA Today*. The *New York Post* was more direct— "GRETZKY: DEVILS ARE MICKEY MOUSE TEAM."

"You'd have thought I'd criticized Miss Newark or something," said Gretzky. "The fans went crazy against me. In retrospect, I probably shouldn't have said it."

Nevertheless, the words had been spoken and, by repetition, gained currency. It is the law of sensational journalism. If you have a good angle, ride it, ride it, ride it, until the opposition drops it first.

What Gretzky didn't bargain for was that the Devils and their fans would seize upon Mickey Mouse and toss his image back at them on January 15, 1984. That was when the Oilers would confront New Jersey for the first time since The Great One uttered his deathless Mickey Mouse slur.

Before the game even started, Gretzky scanned the stands and understood what he had done. Fans were wearing Mickey Mouse ears and carrying signs, "GRETZKY IS GOOFY."

A classic of its kind, the contest ended with a 5-4 Edmonton victory, but for the Devils it was, as *Edmonton Sun* writer Dick Chubey put it, "a moral victory."

IV
Incredible Feats/ Personalities

58 | HOW A LONG-SHOT HORSE BET TURNED TORONTO INTO A WINNING TEAM

When **Conn Smythe** took control of the Toronto Maple Leafs at the end of the 1920s, he badly needed a star defenseman to make the club a winner. Told that the Ottawa Senators would unload King Clancy for $35,000 cash and a couple of players, Smythe wanted to make the move.

There was one issue to be solved, though; he didn't have the money. What he did have was a racehorse named Rare Jewel and an upcoming Coronation Stakes for Canadian-bred two year olds.

Smythe decided to take the gamble and enter Rare Jewel into the race, although the experts said it didn't have a chance. Author Anne M. Logan, who authored a tribute to Clancy, recalled the events leading up the race.

"Various coincidences convinced Smythe this might be his big break in racing; he was also notoriously lucky in his gambling," wrote Logan in *Rare Jewel For A King: A Tribute to King Clancy.*

"The horse was number seven on the card and her pole position as eleven; seven come eleven had to be good. He took some loyal pals to the track with him—Ivan Mikailoff, the wrestling promoter, business associate Ed Bickle, Hugh Aird, Larkin Maloney, and

Fred Crawford—and along with Smythe, they totaled the entire wagers on Rare Jewel.

"It was reported a typical Woodbine opening, with a crowd estimated at twelve to fifteen thousand. There were two or three showers, which settled the dust, and by the time of the Stakes race all was clear again."

The *Toronto Telegram* newspaper explained how a long shot, at 107-1 odds, managed to come through, thanks to jockey Due Foden, who believed in Rare Jewel.

"Foden," noted the *Telegram*, had much to do with the result. "He slipped his filly on the rail at the home turn, and before Baker, on Forth Blower, realized it, he was barging out in front with Rare Jewel a couple of lengths to the good. Forth Blower set sail after her and just failed to get up. J. P. White's Roche D'or, as great an outsider as Rare Jewel, ran third. Rare Jewel won by half a length over the favorite."

The odds were 107-1, paying $214.40 on a $2.00 bet, $46.75 to place, and $19.95 to show. This totaled over $12,000 to Smythe, with $3,570 for the winner's purse and $9,372.70 for his bet. It was also the first time his blue and white colors were paraded, and it remained as the largest mutual price paid in Canada in 1930.

When he was congratulated by P. J. Mulqueen, all he could think of was: "Now we can buy Clancy. Now we are going to win the Stanley Cup."

With the dough, Smythe gave the Senators $35,000, along with forward Eric Pettinger and defenseman Art Smith—total value $15,000—for Clancy. Sure enough, the Leafs had the cornerstone of a powerhouse and went on to win the Cup in 1932. The acquisition of Clancy also enabled Smythe to round up enough money to build Maple Leaf Gardens, which would be *the* jewel of all NHL arenas at that time.

And it all happened because of a horse named Rare Jewel that went off to 107-1 odds.

Or, as hockey journalist Jordan Schoem remarked: "Clancy that!"

59 | THE ULTIMATE CASE OF RUBBER-ITIS—AND AN INCREDIBLE SAVE AT SEA

When goaltenders are overwhelmed with too many shots in a game, it has been said that they suffer from "Rubber-itis," as in too many 6-ounce, vulcanized chunks of rubber being hurled at them.

The ultimate case of "Rubber-itis" befell a goaltender named Sam Lopresti. On the night of March 4, 1941, Sam Lopresti guarded the Chicago Black Hawk net at Boston Garden and faced an incredible 83 shots on goal! Frank Brimsek, the Boston netminder that night, faced only 18 shots the entire game, while Lopresti met a barrage of 36 pucks in the first period alone, followed by 26 shots in the second and 21 in the third.

More amazing than the amount of shots on goal was the amount Lopresti directed out of danger that night. Only three goals got beyond Lopresti, and it wasn't until a late third period score by Bruin Eddie Wiseman that the game was decided. The final score: Boston 3, Chicago 2.

"The Bruins didn't get the winning goal until the end of the game," Lopresti once recalled from his tavern in Minnesota. "Wiseman got it on a rebound. But we couldn't do anything right from the opening faceoff; just couldn't move the puck out of our zone. They were shooting from every angle, and I didn't see half the shots. They were bouncing off my pads, chest protector, my arms, my shoulders. I didn't even know where they were coming from. I lost between eight and 10 pounds that night."

After his second big-league season the same year, Lopresti faced the 83-shot barrage, he joined the United States Navy on the theory that, "it was safer to face Nazi U-boats in the North Atlantic than vulcanized rubber in North America."

Goalie LoPresti was now in the Armed Guard section of the Navy. Instead of fending off rubber, Sam manned a lone gun on a merchant ship, SS *Roger B*. Tahey, which ferried supplies across to England. This time, LoPresti was fending off enemy planes. But on February 7, 1943, Sam's ship was torpedoed. As fire spread across the decks, a second German torpedo sunk the ship.

Sam and twenty-eight other men were packed in one lifeboat with minimal food and water. Remarkably, they spent forty-two days at sea and were only able to do so after LoPresti dove overboard. The goalie somehow managed to lash his sheath knife to a boat hook and stabbed a 35-pound dolphin from which the sailors actually drank blood to sustain themselves.

They sailed 2,500 miles before being picked up off the coast of Brazil; one of the longest open boat voyages in history. LoPresti and his mates were revived in a Santos, Brazil, hospital. Sam, who never played in the NHL again, eventually returned to the ice playing minor league hockey until 1951. LoPresti died in 1984. He had the pleasure of watching his son, Pete, play six seasons of big-league hockey through the 1970s and the 1980-81 season.

60 | THEY SAID IT COULDN'T BE DONE AND YET IT WAS DONE—BUT ONLY ONCE!

I n the ninety-six-year history of the National Hockey League, only one team ever has lost the first three games of the Stanley Cup Final and then rebounded to capture the next four contests and win The Stanley Cup.

It happened in the spring of 1942 and the Toronto Maple Leafs were the team that wrote history that never has been rewritten.

How could such a once-in-a-hockey-lifetime event have taken place?

The answer can be found in several factors which, incredibly, perfectly fell into place to doom the Detroit Red Wings and eventually help the Maple Leafs win the prize.

To begin with, the Leafs, coached by Hap Day, were favored to win the Cup since they finished 15 points ahead of the Motor City sextet, coached by Jack Adams. Plus, Toronto boasted high-scoring sniper Gordie Drillon, a future Hall of Famer, and rugged defenseman Wilfed (Bucko) McDonald fronting for another Hall of Famer, Turk Broda in goal.

Yet, to the astonishment of practically everybody, Detroit won the first three straight games and seemed prepared for a four-game sweep before the home crowd at Olympia Stadium.

It was then that Day played a game of hockey roulette, taking one gamble after another and winning them all.

His first unbelievable decision was to bench his leading scorer, Drillon, and crack defenseman, McDonald. Drillon's slot was filled by utility skater Don Metz while an inexperienced defenseman, Ernie Dickens, replaced McDonald. A second freshman backliner, Bob Goldham, also was added to the Toronto varsity.

But Day's bag of tricks still had a surprise or two more and one was a letter he had received from a fourteen-year-old girl. With the missive in hand, he read her encouraging message to the troops in the visitors' dressing room as the Leafs prepared for the fourth game.

By the time Day had finished reading the letter, every one of his players was inspired for action. "Don't worry about this one, Skipper," shouted veteran forward Dave (Sweeney) Schriner, "we'll win this one for the little girl." Then, Billy (The Kid) Taylor shouted, "We're not licked yet."

And they were not licked; but it was close.

Before a roaring standing room crowd, Detroit took a 2-0 lead but—as promised by Taylor and Schriner—the Leafs fought back, and with less than eight minutes remaining, Nick Metz broke a 3-3 tie with the game-winner, on passes from Syl Apps and Nick's kid brother, the utility man, Don Metz.

Then another key element fell into place—in Toronto's favor. Displeased by the officiating, Red Wings coach Jack Adams leaped over the boards at the end of the game and rained punches on referee Mel Harwood. When the dust had cleared, a witness, NHL president Frank Calder, suspended Adams indefinitely. Now Detroit was without a head coach but with a three-games-to-one lead.

Meanwhile, Day wasn't through with his surprises. Before Game Five, he promoted nineteen-year-old left wing Gaye

Stewart, although the rookie was less than a year out of Junior hockey. Stewart replaced three-year veteran Hank Goldup. On the Red Wings side, veteran Ebbie Goodfellow—no longer useful as a player—took over as interim coach.

Revived and returned to Maple Leaf Gardens for Game Five, the Leafs dominated. What's more, the heretofore unknown Don Metz scored a three-goal hat trick as Toronto triumphed 9-3. And so it was back to Detroit as the Leafs became believers in themselves. Especially Don Metz, who this time scored the winning goal as the Leafs tied the series at three games apiece.

When the game ended, a Detroit fan threw a dead fish on the ice. "That dead fish," wrote Toronto publicist Ed Fitkin, "seemed to be symbolic of the Red Wings fans' reaction to the collapse of their team."

The seventh and final game was played on the night of April 18, 1942, at Maple Leaf Gardens, where 16,240 spectators set a record as the largest crowd in Canadian hockey history to that point in time.

Stunned to the very core by the Maple Leafs comeback, the visiting Detroiters nevertheless rallied and took a 1-0 lead on Syd Howe's goal. It remained that way until the third period when Schriner tied the count, sending the audience into transports of joy. But a tie was not enough and Day brainstormed to find a winning combination. Finally, he sent young center Pete Langelle on left wing with veteran Bob Davidson and Johnny McCreedy on the right side. With the exception of Davidson, the others were regarded as light scorers.

Immediately, they stormed into the Detroit zone with McCreedy leading the way. Johnny took a shot at Detroit goalie Johnny Mowers who moved far out of his cage to cut down the angle. He stopped the puck, but it rebounded back into play, leaving Mowers stranded away from his gaping net. In a desperate lunge, the Detroit defense tried to cover the abandoned goal, but Langelle pounced on the puck like a tiger capturing its prey and smacked it into the cage.

At last, the Leafs were ahead and weren't prepared to stop there. With less than five minutes remaining, Schriner proved to be Ole Reliable and clinched the contest with another goal. As the overhead clock ticked away the remaining seconds, the crowd helped it along until reciting in loud unison the final *"five . . . four . . . three . . . two . . . one!!"*

And the bell sounded to end the most remarkable—call it unreal—Stanley Cup Final of all-time!

61 | HE SCORED A GOAL, BUT NOT WITH HIS STICK: HOW COME?

ho says you have to have your own hockey stick to score a goal?

Not if your name is Bobby Ryan and you're playing for the Anaheim Ducks during the 2011-12 season.

This strange but true feat actually happened during a game at Honda Center between the Ducks and Minnesota Wild in what was a record-breaking game in many ways.

Eventual Rocket Richard and Hart Trophy winner Corey Perry scored his first career hat trick (en route to a career-high 50-goal season), and marked only the second time an Anaheim player has earned such an honor in three different ways: at even strength, on a short-handed penalty shot, and on the power play. The "RPG" line of Bobby Ryan, Corey Perry, and Ryan Getzlaf was on fire, combining for a whopping 11 points on the night.

But Perry, at least, scored all three of his goals with his own stick.

Three minutes after Perry doubled his evening tally, the Wild found themselves tied up deep in their own end, wrangling for the puck in the left corner. Suddenly lacking a stick, Minnesota Wild captain Mikko Koivu grabbed Bobby Ryan's stick right out

Bobby Ryan (front) scored a goal for the Ducks in an unorthodox fashion. *AP Photo/Mike Fuentes*

of his hands. As the players emerged from the corner, a newly-stickless Ryan had to do some quick thinking of his own.

The Ducks winger noticed Koivu's discarded stick on the ice and—tit-for-tat—figured he was entitled to use it for the time being. Seconds later, Wild goalie Niklas Backstrom kicked the rebound of a Toni Lydman shot from the point out to an undefended Bobby Ryan, who promptly one-timed the puck into the empty net for his number 14 goal of the season. A gleeful Ryan immediately mock-saluted his adversary with the borrowed stick as a shocked and surly Koivu looked on. What's even more incredible is that Ryan is a right-handed shot—and he was using Koivu's left-handed stick!

62 | HOW "THE CAPTAIN" DELIVERED ON HIS GUARANTEE

Rescuing a team from the brink of elimination is heroic. However, guaranteeing it beforehand is truly incredible.

In the 1994 Eastern Conference Final, the New York Rangers trailed the New Jersey Devils three games to two, and faced an elimination game in the Meadowlands. The Blueshirts, who hadn't won Lord Stanley's Cup since 1940, looked all but dead.

Sensing his Rangers needed to regain the confidence that led them to the President's Trophy in the 1993-94 season, captain Mark Messier made a bold prediction, and guaranteed that the Rangers would send the series back to New York for a seventh game.

Despite Messier's confidence, it was the New Jersey sextet who came out flying at the start of Game Six. The Devils dominated the first twenty minutes, and skated off the ice with a 2-0 lead on the strength of goals by Scott Niedermayer and Claude Lemieux.

New Jersey's domination carried into the second period, and if it weren't for the great goaltending of Rangers' netminder Mike Richter, the Devils would have extended their lead. The Rangers' bleak situation hit rock bottom midway through the period, when head coach Mike Keenan called a timeout, and didn't say a single word.

However, whatever Keenan didn't say seemed to jumpstart the Blueshirts. With less than three minutes to play in the frame, Messier carried the puck into New Jersey's zone, and passed the puck to Alexei Kovalev. The Russian winger fired a slap shot past the Devils' Martin Brodeur and cut New Jersey's lead to the slimmest of margins.

Kovalev's goal sparked the New York sextet, who came out flying in the third period. Now, it was time for Messier to make good on his promise.

On a rush up the ice, Kovalev hit Messier with a pass, and the Rangers' captain took a wrist shot that beat Brodeur on the short side to tie the game.

Midway through the period, with the teams skating four aside, the Blueshirts once again charged into New Jersey territory. Brodeur stopped Kovalev's initial shot, but Messier found the rebound and scored to give the Rangers a 3-2 lead.

The curtain call came with less than two minutes to play in regulation. With the Devils on a power play, Brodeur skated to the bench to give New Jersey a six-on-four advantage.

With the puck in the Rangers zone, Messier intercepted John MacLean's centering pass, and looked toward the vacant Devils net. The Rangers' captain fired the puck the length of the ice, hitting the center of the net to complete the natural hat trick.

The Rangers would go on to win the series and the Stanley Cup. Although Messier won five Stanley Cups with the Edmonton Oilers, he is known more for his triumph in New York, thanks in large part to his guarantee.

63 | THE IMPOSSIBLE ONE-MAN SCORING SPURT—THREE GOALS IN 21 SECONDS

The United States Marines have had a slogan, "The difficult we do immediately. The impossible takes a little longer."

For Chicago Blackhawks sniper Bill "Wee Willie" Mosienko, the "impossible scoring feat"—three goals in less than a minute—actually only took 21 seconds.

The astonishing one-man performance occurred on March 23, 1952, at Madison Square Garden. It was the final game of the season of a team so dismal that management closed the entire upper balcony section and allowed all five thousand of the diehards to sit in the lower arena for the Rangers-Chicago game.

What they saw was extraordinary. To begin with, the two top New York goalies, Charlie Rayner and Emile Francis, both had been sidelined with injuries. The substitute was skinny Lorne Anderson, a twenty-year-old who had actually won and lost the first two games he had played for the Blueshirts. For a time, it appeared that he would win again. The Rangers had built a three-goal cushion over the Hawks heading into the final period.

Then a hockey miracle happened. With both teams at full strength, Mosienko beat Anderson at 6:09 of the third period. He then lined up with Gus Bodnar at center ice. Bodnar won the draw

It will never happen again—three goals by one player in 21 seconds. Chicago Blackhawks captain Bill (Wee Willie) Mosienko accomplished the feat against the Rangers in March, 1952./*ASSOCIATED PRESS*

and dished a pass to Mosienko, who beat the Rangers defense and flipped the puck past Anderson at 6:20. Mosie had scored twice in 11 seconds.

He and Bodnar lined up again and executed virtually the same play. The pass went to Mosienko, and 10 seconds later, he had deked Anderson for his third goal in 21 seconds.

Hard as it may be to believe, the Bodnar-Mosienko duet combined again—and there was Mosienko skating in alone on Anderson. For a split second, it appeared as if he had scored his fourth goal within 30 seconds, but his shot hit the post and Mosienko skated to the bench where his coach Ebbie Goodfellow barked, "Whatsa matter, Mosie, are you in a slump?"

Ignominiously, the Rangers lost the game, 7-6.

64 | HOCKEY FIRST, SLEEP LATER

In the early days of the Eastern Amateur Hockey League, tight scheduling was not uncommon. But no team was more victimized by games played than the Baltimore Orioles.

The scheduling frenzy once peaked when the Orioles played a tough game in Hershey, Pennsylvania, on a Saturday night. The team subseqeuntly returned to Baltimore at three in the morning the same night.

There was precious little time to sleep, since they had to catch a train back to New York for a Sunday afternoon game against the St. Nicholas Club at Madison Square Garden.

Hockey writer Sam Gunst of Baltimore remembered the scene in New York. "So exhausted were the boys that Sunday afternoon in New York between periods they dozed on the floor of their dressing room. But they were extremely wide-awake on the ice, beating a powerful St. Nick's club, 4–3."

65 | HATS OFF, DEREK! — HOW A ROOKIE DID THE IMPOSSIBLE IN HIS NHL DEBUT

For most National Hockey League players, scoring one goal in their debut would be memorable. To score three would appear to be too unrealistic.

However, New York Rangers center Derek Stepan made the impossible a reality on the night of October 9, 2010.

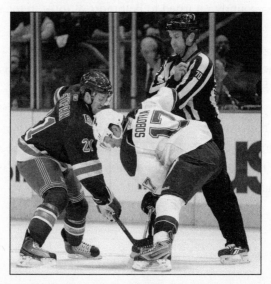

How about that Derek Stepan (left) of the Rangers? The rookie center delivered a three-goal hat trick in his very first NHL game, on October 9, 2010./ *David Perlmutter*

Stepan's NHL debut came during the Rangers' season opener against the Sabres in Buffalo. The twenty-year-old center, who had completed two seasons of college hockey at the University of Wisconsin, wasn't even sure if he would make the Rangers varsity out of training camp.

The rookie's first goal came just over halfway through the first period. Rangers' defenseman Dan Girardi took a shot from the blue line that Stepan deflected. The puck pinballed off of Sabres' defenseman Tyler Myers and slid past goalie Ryan Miller.

Stepan's second tally came with under five minutes remaining in the second period. Miller made a save on Marc Staal's shot, but Stepan buried the rebound to give the Blueshirts a 3-1 lead.

Before the period was over, Stepan had completed his memorable night. Sean Avery held the puck behind the net, and centered the puck to a wide-open Stepan in front of the net. The rookie took the pass and beat Miller before the goalie had a chance to react.

66 | RED KELLY–THE MOST ASTONISHING TRANSFORMATION

Because hockey is the fastest team game on earth it has been perfectly natural for some exceptional older forwards—in their waning years—to try their luck on defense.

An excellent example of one such transformation was accomplished by Neil Colville of the New York Rangers. For years he had starred as a forward on the Blueshirts crack scoring line along with his brother Mac and Alex Shibicky. The trio starred during the 1940 New Yorkers march to the Stanley Cup.

When World War II broke out, Neil Colville enlisted in the Canadian Armed Forces and returned to the Big Apple when the conflict ended. Having lost his speed over the years, Neil moved back to defense and was so proficient that he was named to the National Hockey League's Second All-Star Team for the 1947-48 season.

But nobody in NHL history did it the other way around in the sensational manner of Leonard (Red) Kelly, who transformed from a Cup-winning Hall of Fame defenseman into a Cup-winning forward.

A tobacco farmer in his native Simcoe, Ontario, in the off-season, Kelly broke into hockey's major league with the Detroit

Red Wings in the 1947-48 season. Kelly emerged as a top-flight rushing defenseman who often led the attack like Bobby Orr long before the flashy Boston Bruins ace came along.

Teaming with such notables as Gordie Howe, Ted Lindsay, and Sid Abel, Kelly helped the Motor City sextet to four Stanley Cup championships before his boss, manager Jack Adams, deemed him expendable. Early in the 1960s, Adams traded Kelly—along with forward Billy McNeill—to the Rangers for defenseman Bill Gadsby and forward Eddie Shack.

To the surprise of the hockey world, Kelly adamantly refused to report to New York and, in effect, retired from hockey. Finally, after a few weeks of behind-the-scenes wrangling, the deal was revoked and, instead, Kelly was traded to the Toronto Maple Leafs for defenseman Marc Reaume in February 1960.

Most observers believed that this was the beginning of the end for Red but, actually, it turned out to be a new beginning. George (Punch) Imlach, the Maple Leafs manager and coach, detected something in Kelly that eluded everyone else in the NHL and converted Red to a center man. At first it seemed like a bizarre experiment that would end as quickly as it had been formulated, especially since Red was up in his years.

Kelly washed up? Not a chance. Centering for the likes of Frank (Big M) Mahovlich and Bob Nevin, Red became one of the premier NHL pivots and regenerated the Toronto offense, turning the Maple Leafs into a three-straight Cup-winning team (1962, 1963, 1964), before they added a fourth in 1967.

Remarkably, Kelly did just as well up front with the Leafs as he had on the back line with Detroit. Before hanging up his skates Red had won four Stanley Cups as a center in Toronto to match the quartet he had earned on defense with Detroit.

No other hockey player can make that statement! Nor will any in the future.

67 | LEO REISE, JR.: A DEFENSEMAN WITH A STRATEGIC OFFENSE

During the 1940s, it was rare for a defenseman to score many goals. In the 1949-50 season, Detroit Red Wings backliner, Leo Reise, managed four red lights over 70 games; and that was considered a lot for Leo, who tallied five goals in 1948-49 and did it again in 1950-51.

A defensive defenseman, Leo Reise, Jr. stunned the Toronto Maple Leafs goalie Turk Broda in the 1950 playoffs by scoring two sudden-death goals in two straight games./*ASSOCIATED PRESS*

But it was in a seven-game series between his Red Wings and the Toronto Maple Leafs in the spring of 1950 when Reise turned into a spectacular scoring machine. During Game 4, on April 4, 1950, with his club trailing Toronto 2-1 in games, Reise saved his mates. With the score tied 1-1, the game surged into double overtime when Reise fired the game-winner past goalie Turk Broda.

But Leo's heroics didn't stop there. The series went to a seventh and final game at Detroit's Olympia Stadium. And this time, the series would be decided by the first goal because it was tied at 0-0 after 60 minutes. Remarkably, Reise rose to the occasion once again, firing a blueline blast past a screened Broda at 8:34 of the sudden-death period.

That made it two pivotal sudden-death goals in one series for Leo, who went on to win a Cup for Detroit in a seven-game final against the New York Rangers in 1950. Interestingly, Reise did not collect a single point—neither a goal nor an assist—in that seven-game Cup final series against New York.

68 | SOMEONE WHO ACTUALLY PLAYED FOR SEVERAL HOCKEY TEAMS, A BASKETBALL CLUB, AND THE BROOKLYN DODGERS

During the late 1930s and into the 1940s and 1950s, there was a sports trivia question to end all New York sports trivia questions.

It was, "Who played for the New York Rangers, New York Rovers, New York Knickerbockers, and the Brooklyn Dodgers?"

Admittedly, it was a toughie, unless you happened to know that Gladys Goodding was the house organist at Madison Square Garden as well as Ebbets Field, home of the baseball Dodgers.

Miss Goodding not only was an accomnplished jazz organist, but also a sports fan who connected tunes with teams. For example, when the Blackhawks played the Rangers, Gladys would hit the keys with the classic tune, "Chicago." Likewise, when the Detroit skaters took the ice before an MSG game, Goodding would pump out "Pretty Red Wing."

She did likewise for the Sunday afternoon Rovers games and played "Easter Parade" for the home team on the grounds that the Rovers usually made the playoffs around Easter Sunday.

Gladys also was there for Metropolitan League contests and each club in the local circuit had its own song. My favorite belonged to the Sands Point Tigers—"Hold That Tiger."

As for the Rangers, well, that was easy. Popular New York tunesmith J. Fred Coots had taken care of that just about when Gladys went to work for the Blueshirts. It was called "The Rangers Victory Song" and, believe it or not, the sheet music still exists.

69 | DON'T MESS WITH THE ROCKET

When Maurice "Rocket" Richard was starring for the Montreal Canadiens in the 1940s and 1950s, he also could have been nicknamed the Muhammad Ali of the ice. The Rocket not only could score with his stick, but with his fists as well.

In one period of one memorable game on the night of December 17, 1944, the Rocket decked one of hockey's best fighters—not once—but twice in the same period. The victim was Bob "Killer" Dill, whose other claim to fame was the fact that he was a nephew of Mike and Tom Gibbons, both famous in a fistic game.

Like many other opponents of Richard, the strategy was to antagonize the Montreal ace until he retaliated. Both players would then be penalized, but at least Richard would be off the ice. That is precisely what Dill seemed to have in mind on that night in 1944. Dill challenged Richard a few seconds after Chuck Scherza of the Rangers and Leo Lamoureux of the Canadiens had started their own private war. Up until then, Dill had been reputed to be one of the toughest skaters to come down the pike. In the first bout, Richard disposed of Dill with a hefty right to the jaw.

When the Ranger recovered, referee King Clancy sent him to the penalty box with a major penalty for fighting and doled out the same sentence to Richard. Penalty benches, in those days, were constructed without a barrier separating the players of opposing teams, so it was not unusual for the combatants to exchange insults while they awaited their release. Still smarting from his knockout, Dill challenged Richard to a return bout. Maurice, a French-Canadian who spoke virtually no English whatsoever, didn't quite understand Dill's monologue, but there was no mistaking the Ranger's sign language.

Dill tossed the first punch, and the two were off and swinging on the dry wood of the penalty box. By chance, Dan Daniel of the *New York World-Telegram*, who had covered boxing in his day as a reporter, was watching the bout. "Maurice The Mauler again measured his man," wrote Daniel. "Roberto [Dill] suffered a cut left eye and other bruises and contusions." Another described it as, "the most interesting wartime set-to on local ice."

The pickling of Dill was finally summed up by another boxing writer who noted: "Richard scored two widely separated but emphatic knockdowns. And he won on points!"

Maurice (The Rocket) Richard was considered the Babe Ruth of hockey, but he could fight as well as he could score. *ASSOCIATED PRESS*

70 | ART COULTER: A HERO FOR THE RANGERS—A HERO FOR THE COAST GUARD

One of the most incredible double-dip championship runs for an athlete was enjoyed by Art Coulter, a defenseman who helped the Chicago Blackhawks to a Stanley Cup Championship in 1934 and later captained the New York Rangers to the Cup in 1940.

But Coulter didn't stop there. After the United States entered World War II, Coulter enlisted in the US Coast Guard and was stationed at the Guard's Curtis Bay Yard in Baltimore, Maryland. As it happened, the Coast Guard at Curtis Bay formed a hockey team comprised of former NHL players such as Johnny Mariucci of the Blackhawks and Frankie "Mr. Zero" Brimsek of the Boston Bruins.

Playing in the Eastern League, the Cutters played in both the 1942-43 and 1943-44 seasons while Coulter guided the Coast Guard skaters to two Championships before doing his tour of duty.

71 | A RECORD THAT CAN NEVER–EVER–BE BROKEN, THANKS TO BUTCH GORING

When the New York Islanders became a power-house in the late 1970s, they were powered by a Hall of Fame line comprised of Mike Bossy, Bryan Trottier, and Clark Gillies. Their primary goalie Bill Smith also became as Hall of Famer as well as defenseman Denis Potvin.

Despite this wealth of talent, the Islanders were upset in the 1978 playoffs by an inferior Toronto Maple Leafs team in a brutally vicious seven-game preliminary playoff series and—again a year later—by an underdog Rangers team which beat the Nassau skaters in six games.

Bill Torrey, the Islanders general manager, was besieged with complaints. Some called his club "choke artists," while others called for the firing of coach Al Arbour. Torrey resisted the critics and on the deadline for trading in March 1980, he dealt forward Bill Harris—his original first overall draft pick—and defenseman Dave Lewis to the Los Angeles Kings, for center Butch Goring.

Nobody could foresee the result of the exchange at the time but within days the entire chemistry of the Islanders changed. Goring not only emerged as a superstar but took the load off Trottier, giving the Isles a pair of crack pivots and, even better, a Stanley Cup in 1980. Not only did the Isles repeat the feat in 1981, but

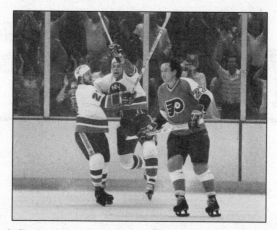

Butch Goring (left, helmeted) became an Islander in a late-season trade during the 1979-1980 season. Goring helped lead the Islanders to four straight Stanley Cups./*AP Photo/Ray Stubblebine*

Goring won the Conn Smythe Trophy as the most valuable player in the playoffs.

"Butch was the player who turned our club from pretenders to contenders," said Glenn (Chico) Resch, who was goaltender for the Islanders when they won the 1980 Cup. "He enabled that club to do what no other has done before or since."

What Resch meant was that the Islanders—with Goring and Trottier leadng the way—won *nineteen consecutive playoff rounds*—and a total of four Stanley Cups, before the Edmonton Oilers defeated them in the Spring of 1984.

"Without Goring," Resch concluded, "it never could have happened."

Yet the irony of all Islanders ironies is that Butch never made it to the Hockey Hall of Fame.

However, he did make it to the club's broadcast booth, where he now is an analyst for the Madison Square Garden Network's Isles telecasts!

72 THE COACH WITH A TRIFECTA OF CHAMPIONSHIPS—GENTLEMAN JOE PRIMEAU

I t often has been said that nice guys don't last when it comes to coaching in professional hockey's big league.

Or, as one player-turned-broadcaster put it, "You have to be a real *S.O.B* if you want to run the bench and also win titles."

Though there have been notable exceptions, just one—and only one—coach proved that he could do it right across the board and win championships in three leagues.

That would be Joe Primeau, a native of Lindsay, Ontario, who starred at center for the Toronto Maple Leafs, starting in 1929. Primeau was pivotal for one of the finest forward units in National Hockey League annals. His right wing was Charlie Conacher, while Busher Jackson patrolled the port side. The press dubbed them "The Kid Line" and they underlined their ability by spearheading the Leafs to Toronto's first Stanley Cup in 1932. That same year, Primeau's clean play prompted the league to award him the Lady Byng Trophy. Appropriately, he earned the monicker Gentleman Jim.

After retiring as a player in 1936, Primeau went into the perilous job of coaching. His first job was on the junior level, working behind the bench for St. Michael's College School—which is actually a high school—in Toronto. Primeau guided St. Mike's to the

Memorial Cup, emblematic of Canada's junior championship, in 1945. That team nurtured several future Hall of Famers, and in 1946, his club reached the final Game Seven before being taken by the Winnipeg Monarchs.

Then, the Primeau-guided St. Mike's club won another Memorial Cup in 1947. Maple Leafs boss Conn Smythe was so impressed, that he hired Gentleman Joe to coach the Toronto Marlboros, a "Senior" team during an era when "Senior" hockey was just a cut below the major league level.

Unstoppable at the senior level, Primeau sipped champagne from the Allan Cup, "senior" hockey's equivalent of the Stanley Cup, in 1949 and again in 1950.

When Clarence (Hap) Day retired as Maple Leafs coach—he already had five Stanley Cup rings—Primeau was signed to coach his first NHL club. Day admittedly was a hard act to follow, but Primeau was unfazed. After a strong second-place finish, his Toronto sextet reached the Finals and disposed of the Montreal Canadiens in five games, all of which were settled in sudden-death overtime.

Thus, Gentleman proved that nice guys can finish on top, and he had the un-real honor of a championship hat trick!

73 | FROM STAIRWAY TO STARDOM

Jaromir Jagr is arguably the best Czech-born player to have skated in the National Hockey League. And one of the reasons why he got that way was from running up and down stairs—to build up his leg muscles. For example, whenever he played a road or home game he would precede his morning practice by running to the top of every arena staircase that he could.

It wasn't the only reason why the native of Kladno, Czech Republic, helped Pittsburgh to win two Stanley Cups and later starred for Washington, New York, and Philadelphia. But Jags would tell you it surely didn't hurt.

Former Ranger, Jaromir Jagr, who helped guide the Boston Bruins to the 2013 Stanley Cup Final, was one of the most intensely-trained players of all-time. One of his favorite exercises was running up and down stairs in every NHL arena./*David Perlmutter*

74 | STAAL, STAAL, AND STAAL

No, it's not a law firm. Staal, Staal, and Staal represent one of the most successful hockey families in NHL history. The first to make it big in The Show was center iceman Eric (second overall pick in the 2003 NHL Entry Draft) for the Carolina Hurricanes, eventually powering the team to a Stanley Cup Championship in the 2005-06 season.

He was followed by defenseman Marc Staal—who was also a first round pick (twelfth overall)—in the 2005 NHL Entry Draft. Marc matured into one of the New York Rangers' best backliners.

One year later, Jordan, also a center, was Pittsburgh's first-round choice in 2006 (second overall) in the NHL Entry Draft and helped the Penguins win a Cup in 2009. In 2012, Jordan was traded to Carolina to play alongside his older brother, Eric.

The NHL has had a tradition of several family members skating in the majors. The Chicago Blackhawks had three Bentley brothers (all forwards)—Max, Doug, and Reg. Both Max and Doug are in the Hockey Hall of Fame. Another interesting family grouping featured defenseman Muzz Patrick and left wing Lynn Patrick, skating on the 1940 Stanley Cup-winning New York Rangers. The manager of that team just happened to be their father, the legendary Silver Fox, Lester Patrick.

Interestingly, that same Rangers team featured another brother act, Mac and Neil Colville, who together with Alex Shibickey comprised one of the NHL's best forward units.

75

WHO'S MEL HILL? CHECK OUT "SUDDEN DEATH," AND YOU'LL FIND OUT!

When the 1939 Stanley Cup semifinal round between the New York Rangers and Boston Bruins was about to begin at Madison Square Garden, the Beantowners were favored to take Lord Stanley's mug. Starting with Frankie (Mister Zero) Brimsek in goal, coach Art Ross' club was loaded with future Hall of Famers.

Up front, for example, there were such future Hall of Famers as Bill Cowley and Roy Conacher, not to mention all three members of the Kraut Line—Milt Schmidt, Bobby Bauer, and Woody Dumart.

Buried down the roster was a right wing named Melvin John Hill out of an obscure Manitoba village called Glenboro. Mel Hill scored ten goals that season for Boston, which was just fine for a third-liner since nothing more was expected of him. Nor was anything much anticipated when the puck was dropped for the opening face-off at the Garden on March 21, 1939.

Rangers coach Lester (The Silver Fox) Patrick instructed his players to keep an Argus eye on the ever-dangerous Krauts, along with playmaking ace Cowley and notorious sharpshooter Conacher whose older brother Charlie had been a dominant scorer in Toronto. As far as Patrick was concerned, there was no need to focus on Hill.

Error!

Game One was tied at one goal apiece after regulation time, reflective of what would be a tightly played best-of-seven series.

The first overtime period left the game still deadlocked, 1-1, as did the second sudden death. Once in the dressing room, coach Ross sat down with Cowley and came up with a plan. Since the Rangers still were shadowing Krauts and Conacher, they might be overlooking Hill.

"Feed Mel," Ross insisted. "Maybe we'll fool them."

For more than 19 minutes of the third overtime, nobody was fooling anybody and it appeared that in less than 40 seconds, the teams would retire to prepare for a *fourth* overtime. But the 20-minute extra session wasn't over, and with less than a minute remaining Cowley skated over the Rangers' blue line, closely watched by hulking New York defenseman Murray (Muzz) Patrick.

Getting a jump on Patrick, Cowley executed an end run that led him into the corner of the rink from where he dished a perfect pass to Hill, conveniently stationed outside the crease guarded by goalie Davey Kerr. Before anyone could say "fourth overtime," Hill deposited the biscuit behind Kerr, and Boston had won 2-1. For those interested, the new day had already begun. It was 1:10 a.m. when Hill began earning what would be a lifetime nickname.

In Game Two, on March 23, 1939, at Boston Garden, the teams again battled through three periods tied; this time it was 2-2. By now Ross had Hill well-ensconced on his second line, along with Cowley at center and Conacher on the left side, which was prescient on the coach's part. At 8:24 of the first overtime, Hill had done it again and Boston took a two-game lead in the series, which was far from over even though Boston won Game Three, 4-1.

The resilient Rangers rebounded with three straight victories, setting up the deciding match on April 2, 1939, on Causeway Street in Boston.

Stunningly, Game Seven was a replica of Game One. The teams were tied 1-1 after regulation and then skirmished for two sudden-death periods without a result. Then came the third overtime, and it was Mel Hill who did it again; only this time only 8 minutes had elapsed before he lit the red light behind Kerr and Boston had won the Stanley Cup.

From that point on, he no longer was known as Mell Hill. The three overtime goals were enough for the press corps to now anoint him "Sudden Death" Hill!

76 | NOT ONLY THE GREATEST, BUT THE ONLY AMBIDEXTROUS SUPERSTAR SCORER

Many experts—not to mention teammates and foes—have considered Gordie Howe as the greatest forward of all time. One witness for Howe was Hall of Fame goalie Harry Lumley.

First a teammate of Howe on the Detroit Red Wings, Lumley later faced him playing goal for the Toronto Maple Leafs. As a puck-stopper, Lumley was often confounded by Howe's ability to shoot equally at ease from the right side or the left.

"There's no doubt," Lumley asserted, "that Howe was the best all-around player I have ever seen. The thing about Howe that always made it difficult for a goalie was the fact that he was ambidextrous.

"He was always switching from his forehand to his backhand, and a goalie continually had to change angles on him."

Gordie Howe is regarded by many experts as the greatest hockey player of all-time. One of Howe's assets was the unique ability to shoot the puck equally as well from the right side or the left side./ *ASSOCIATED PRESS*

77 | CHARLIE GARDINER—A STUDY IN COURAGE BEYOND THE CALL OF DUTY

Before the advent of the face mask and other protective equipment, it generally was agreed that the goaltender's job was the most difficult in all of professional sports.

Imagine, then, how much more challenging it must have been to remain a star netminder while suffering from what would become a fatal ailment.

Those who covered the National Hockey League in the late 1920s and into the early 1930s marveled at the manner in which Gardiner guarded the twine. A native of Edinburgh, Scotland, Charlie grew up in Canada, signing on with the Blackhawks in 1927. Within four years, he became an NHL All-Star and a year later won the Vezina Trophy as the NHL's best goalie.

Unfortunately, the one prize that continued to elude him was The Stanley Cup, which never had been won by a Chicago team since the Blackhawks were admitted to the NHL. But in the 1933-34 season, the Blackhawks finished second in the American Division and advanced to the final round after eliminating both Montreal teams in succession, the Canadiens and then the Maroons.

To casual viewers, Gardiner appeared to be at the very top of his game. He allowed a trifling 83 goals in 48 games and added no less than ten shutouts to his resume. But something *had* changed.

Known by teammates, the press, and friends as a fun guy, Charlie suddenly had turned morose—and for good reason; he was suffering from a chronic tonsil infection, which worsened as the playoffs wore on to the third and final round.

Determined to win the Cup, Gardiner pressed in as Chicago visited Detroit in the playoff that would decide the champion. Overcoming the pain, Charlie out-goaled his opposite, Wilf Cude, 2-1, in double-overtime at Olympia Stadium and returned with a 4-1 triumph in Game Two, putting the Blackhawks just one victory away from the elusive Cup.

However, the pain wracking the goaltender's body had worsened, and by now coach Lionel Conacher and manager Tommy Gorman were aware of the dismal situation. Thinking that he might be replaced, Gardiner made it clear that he would not be removed. "Let me play," he urged, "for the Cup."

This was a request neither Conacher nor Gorman could refuse—and Charlie did play well enough for two-and-a-half periods, keeping the score knotted at 2-2 before Detroit's Doug Young beat him at 13:50 of the third period, spearheading a 5-2 rout.

After returning to the Chicago dressing room, Gardiner—writhing in pain—looked ahead to Game Four and implored his fellow Blackhawks: "All I want is one goal next game. Just one goal, and I'll take care of the other guys."

Two nights later, the Chicago Stadium faithful roared their approval as Charlie led the red-, black-, and white-uniformed skaters on to the ice for what was to be one of the most remarkable games in league history. All Gardiner wanted was that one goal with which to work, but such Chicago marksmen as Doc Romnes, Johnny Gottselig, and Paul Thompson couldn't deliver. And as the first period melded into the second, Charlie's pain-tolerance ebbed, although he blunted every Detroit scoring attempt.

By the end of regulation time, the score was still 0-0 and sudden-death overtime followed. Somehow, the hero goalie had gained a second wind; or so it seemed. Before skating toward the crease he waved his stick to the adoring crowd and continued to match Wilf Cude save for save as the game entered a second extra session.

Meanwhile, Charlie tried every which way to distract himself from the agony that enveloped his body while focusing on enemy shooters. Just as the overhead clock revealed that the second overtime was half over, Chicago's Doc Romnes passed the puck to tiny Harold "Mush" March, who skated over the blue line and sent a wrist shot that baffled Cude. The red light flashed, and Chicago hailed its first Stanley Cup champion.

Saluting the victory, Gardiner tossed his big goalie stick in the air, jubilantly yelled, "Good man, Mush! You've won the Cup!" and was escorted to the winners' dressing room by his appreciative mates.

Alas, the joy was short-lived. Eight weeks later, suffering from uremic convulsions brought on by the tonsil infection of long standing, Gardiner was rushed to a Winnipeg hospital in a state of coma. Late in the day, on Wednesday, June 13, 1934, he died.

78 | HOW PENTTI LUND EXTINGUISHED THE ROCKET'S RED GLARE

During the 1949-50 season, Maurice (The Rocket) Richard was often dubbed "The Babe Ruth of Hockey." To this day, he is regarded as the most exciting goal-scorer of all-time.

The Rocket's Montreal Canadiens were regarded as one the favorites—give or take the Detroit Red Wings—to win the Stanley Cup and the Habs' starry lineup merely underlined the point. Hall of Famers such as Elmer Lach, Ken Reardon, and Bill Durnan graced their lineup while Richard led the National Hockey League in goal-scoring with 43 red lights.

Challenging Montreal in the opening round was a vastly underdog New York Rangers club, which couldn't even make it to the .500 mark that year. The fourth-place Blueshirts finished the regular season with a mediocre mark of 28-31-11, winding up ten points behind the Habs. What made things even gloomier for the Gotham skaters was that their top goal-scorer, Edgar Laprade, managed 22 on the season, 21 fewer than the Rocket.

Rangers coach Lynn Patrick realized that a unique strategy—or, perhaps a miracle—would be necessary to both stifle Richard and beat the Montrealers. After due deliberation with his manager Frank Boucher, Patrick decided that Pentti Lund would "shadow" The Rocket and, hopefully, limit the inimitable one's scoring. Nobody—not even the imaginative Patrick—could have imagined the result.

In fact, Lund once told me during an interview long after he had retired to become sports editor of the Fort William (Ontario) *Daily Times Journal* that not even he himself could have imagined the result. Why would he? After all, Lund's 18 goals during the 1949-50 season were 25 fewer than Richard's.

As big-league hockey players go, Pentti was unique. He was born in Karijoki, Finland, but emigrated to Canada with his family when he was six years old. The Lunds settled in the hockey-mad twin cities of Port Arthur and Fort William, where Pentti became a proficient goal-scorer in the Thunder Bay Hockey League. He enlisted in the Royal Canadian Navy during World War II and also managed to compete with a navy team until the end of hostilities.

A Boston Bruins scout recommended Pentti to the big club and after a tryout, Lund was dispatched to the Boston Olympics, starring for one of the strongest minor league teams on the continent. The Bruins gave him a couple of tryouts before trading Lund to the Rangers, and at the start of the 1948-49 season he became the first Finnish-born player to score a goal in the NHL. It was the first of 14 in 59 games for the affable left wing and helped him win the Calder Trophy as Rookie of the Year. His 16 assists demonstrated that he was an able playmaker as well.

Pentti suffered through a bit of a sophomore slump during the regular part of the 1949-50 campaign, but coach Patrick figured that the line of Lund, Don (Bones) Raleigh, and Ed Slowinski could challenge the Rocket's line, centered with the wizardry of Lach. If ever the odds-makers were thrown for a loss, this New York-Montreal semifinal playoff round had the bookies screaming, "What's going on here?"

To begin with, Lund did such a masterful job on Richard that the Rocket scored one measly goal over the course of the five-game series. By contrast, Pentti scored five big ones to knock multi-Vezina Trophy-winner Durnan out of the goal after three losing games. His replacement, Gerry McNeil, managed one over-time win before the Rangers captured the series four games to one. And it was the Finnish-born Lund who was most responsible for finishing off the Habs in one of the most arresting upsets in Stanley Cup playoff history.

P.S. The Rangers came within a hit goal post from winning the Stanley Cup from Detroit in the first overtime of the decisive seventh game. Although the Blueshirts eventually were defeated in the second sudden-death, they had plenty to cheer about including the heroic Lund, whose 11 points placed him as *the* leading scorer of the entire 1950 playoffs!

79 | THE UN-MASKED GOALIE AND HIS AMAZING RECORD

Some of today's fans find it incredulous that goalies played hockey without a protective facemask. But nobody did it better or for a longer time than Glenn Hall, who played for the Detroit Red Wings, Chicago Blackhawks, and St. Louis Blues.

Most remarkable of all was that Hall played 502 consecutive games after becoming a regular in 1955; or 30,120 successive minutes of goaltending. They didn't call Glenn Hall "Mr. Goalie" for nothing.

A member of the Hockey Hall of Fame, Glenn played in 906 regular season National Hockey League games and 115 play-off contests, totaling 60,383 minutes during which he faced the 6-ounce hunk of vulcanized rubber. Only at the very tail-end of his career did Hall even deign to wear a protective mask, and even then he did so grudgingly. Apart from the sheer brilliance of his style, Hall earned his way into the Hall of Fame because of his remarkable durability.

Hall's exemplary goaltending helped the Chicago Blackhawks to their first Stanley Cup since 1938 when they annexed the mug in 1961. "Nobody came close to Hall when it came to great goaltending," said Hall of Famer Andy Bathgate, who played for the

Rangers, Maple Leafs, and Red Wings. "He was solid in every way. He had a great pair of hands, fast legs, and he played those angles. He was smart—awfully smart—and kept on improving."

Hall's arrival in the Windy City came at a time when the Blackhawks were the NHL's doormat in a six-team league. But Glenn almost single-handedly restored them to respectability, and in 1959-60 Glenn came within two goals of winning the Vezina Trophy. (He was beaten out by Montreal's Jaques Plante.) Two seasons later, Glenn won his first Vezina Trophy. He had developed plenty of good practice since his teammates were Bobby "Golden Jet" Hull and Stan Mikita. Having to face Hull's 100 mph slapshot three times a week in practice had its virtues and drawbacks. "It was tough," said Hall. "Especially when he was younger. Bobby was a brash kid and a little wild on his shots, but as he got older he began to take it easier on me. Anyway, I felt that the practices were overrated by coaches. Ten minutes a day would have been enough for me."

The endless barrage of shots began to take its toll on Hall, and goaltending no longer was the fun that it had once been on the ponds of Humbolt. "It became sixty minutes of hell," he said. "There were many other easier ways of making a living."

In time, Hall became notorious around the NHL as a goaltender who frequently would vomit before the game began. He would refuse to have his photo taken by photographers with flash cameras, on the assumption that it would affect his eyes during a match. "On the one hand, goaltending was stimulating and rewarding, and on the other it was a strain. I would frequently get sick to my stomach, but as bad as it sounded I always felt that the nervousness was part of the game, and its own peculiar way, helped keep me sharp."

The sharpness was evident even after Hall had been traded to the St. Louis Blues. In 1967-68, Glenn played spectacularly as

St. Louis upset the Philadelphia Flyers in a seven-game semi-final and reached the Stanley Cup finals against the Montreal Canadiens. "Strangely enough, I found St. Louis was the easiest team of all to play with, and that goes back to the good Detroit and Chicago clubs. We had a very disciplined defense with Scotty Bowman coaching, a stronger defense than we had in Chicago. At the time, the Blues had good management and the front office knew how to use their players to advantage. Besides that, we were motivated. Players on expansion teams in those days really wanted to prove to the world that they were good enough to play in the NHL."

Late in his career with the Blues, Hall began wearing the type of face mask that Plante originally had introduced when Jacques was a member of the Montreal Canadiens. But Glenn never felt very comfortable with it, looking more like a camel with fins. It was, therefore, appropriate that Hall's retirement was consonant with the widespread use of the mask in both major and minor-league hockey in the early seventies.

Glenn concluded: "I'm sure that somebody would have liked me to continue playing, but my philosophy is that the game should be played real well when you're at you're very best. To me, one hundred percent effort wasn't good enough. Towards the end I began to feel average, and Glenn Hall has always believed that if he is going to do something average, he might as well not do it at all!"

80 | THE MOST STITCHED-UP PLAYER IN HOCKEY WAS ALSO ONE OF THE BEST

Although one of the few areas not covered by the NHL's vast data bank is "stitches absorbed," hockey historians generally agree that Eddie Shore was cut, sliced, punctured, and generally wounded more than any other big-leaguer.

Shore battled his way through a turbulent fifteen-year career that would have driven insurance underwriters to distraction. Dubbed "The Edmonton Express," Shore emerged as one of the NHL's original stars. He launched his NHL stint with the Boston Bruins in 1926, playing a death-defying style of hockey that did absolutely no good for his fuselage.

In a single contest against the hated Montreal Maroons, Shore suffered a lacerated cheekbone, a two-inch cut over his left eye, a broken nose, three broken teeth, and two black eyes. In addition, he was knocked out cold for 14 minutes during the game. Shore did not even miss a step, playing in the following contest.

Another time he broke three ribs after crashing into a goal post. Instead of leaving the Bruins to go to the hospital, Shore slipped away from the doctor, caught a train to Montreal where the next game would be played, and scored two goals the following night!

It has been estimated that Shore was embroidered with more than eight hundred stitches, many being required as a result of fights by Eddie. He set an NHL record for penalty minutes in just his second season in the NHL; despite his reputation as a villain (except in Boston), he was not your typical clumsy goon.

Shore won the Hart Trophy (NHL Most Valuable Player) on four separate occasions and was a first team All-Star seven times. In short, this guy had a knack for playing on the edge and giving up his body to win a game. It proved worthwhile, as he is not only known for his rough and tough style, but his skill, finesse, and winning attitude.

81 | ONE WINNING GOAL PICTURED TWO DIFFERENT WAYS

Andy Hebenton was one of the most remarkable players ever to graduate from the minors to the National Hockey League.

For several seasons in the early 1950s he was buried in the Western Hockey League with the Tacoma Rockets. His coach and manager at the time was Murray "Muzz" Patrick, the former New York Rangers defenseman who played for the 1940 Stanley Cup-winning Blueshirts team. When Muzz became General Manager of the Rangers in 1955, he needed a scorer and remembered how well Hebby had played for him.

It turned out to be a fortuitous move for both Patrick and Hebenton.

Andy played nine consecutive seasons—70 games each—in the NHL without missing a single game. His total was 630 matches without having been sidelined because of injury or incompetence. In 1956-57, Andy won the Lady Byng Trophy while playing for the Rangers, a club for whom he quietly excelled from 1955-56 through 1962-63.

Hebenton's finest hour as a scorer occurred in a 1957 Stanley Cup playoff game when he scored a sudden-death goal at 13:38 in New York's Madison Square Garden against Montreal's Jacques

Plante after eluding defenseman Bob Turner. It was the first overtime playoff game in MSG since 1940 and the Rangers won, 4-3,
although they ultimately lost the series.

Easily the most amusing aspect—from Hebenton's viewpoint—
is the manner in which his winning goal was later depicted.

On the play, Andy sped down the right wing and outflanked
Turner. He then found a small opening between Plante's left pad
and the goalpost to score the winner. The next day photos showed
number twelve scoring the goal one second after the red light
flashed, which was fine.

Next came the tricky part.

During the offseason, the Gold Seal ice cream company
purchased a centerfold, two-page spread in the Rangers program.
Under the headline "Gold Seal Scores" was a picture of Hebenton's
goal. There was only one problem; in the photo accompanying the
ad, Andy was scoring from the left side and wearing number 21.
One could comically say that Hebenton had scored the winning
goal against Plante twice—from the right and left side while
wearing two different numbers.

"I think," said Andy, "the printers made a mistake because I
don't think I was ever good enough to score two sudden-death
goals against Plante at one time!"

V
Outrageous

82 | HOW THE RANGERS PULLED A RE-NAMING FLIMFLAM FOR AN ENTIRE SEASON

When the National Hockey League decided to expand into the Unites States, it was only natural that a team should be placed in the third edition of Madison Square Garden, which opened in 1925. Although the sports palace on Eighth Avenue between Forty-Ninth and Fiftieth Streets originally was not designed for hockey, an ice plant was installed.

Ironically, the first NHL team to represent The Big Apple was not the famed Rangers but rather the former Hamilton (Ontario) Tigers, a club purchased for $500,000 by New York's most notorious bootlegger—prohibition was in full force then—"Big" Bill Dwyer.

The way Dwyer figured it, his team—renamed the Americans—would give him respectability and also make him some money in addition to the millions he was pulling in for bootleg hooch. Sure enough, the Amerks, as New Yorkers loved calling them, proved to be a big hit and turned a profit, although Dwyer had to pay a handsome fee to rent the Garden on hockey nights.

But once the arena's moguls realized that hockey was so popular just one block from The Great White Way, the Garden's owners decided that the arena should have a team that it could call its own. Just a year after the Americans were welcomed to The Big Apple, the Rangers prepared to inaugurate their first major league season. However, there was a problem; the Amerks had cornered the market in fans and even though the term "marketing" had not yet been coined, the Rangers did have to sell their product to the masses. But how?

For starters, the Garden already had a publicist named Johnny Bruno—later to earn fame as the press agent for aviator-hero Charles Lindbergh—and, if nothing else, Bruno was creative. Once Johnny learned that Lester Patrick would be both manager and coach of the new New York entry, he informed the hockey boss that since the Americans had achieved a head start in securing a fan base, the Rangers had to unearth other areas of rooters.

Bruno advised Patrick of the large Jewish and Italian populations in New York and the fact that having a Jewish or Italian player on the team might boost popularity.

When Patrick shot back that there wasn't a single Jew nor an Italian on the roster, Bruno was unmoved and told Lester that he could get around that little obstacle.

After checking through the lineup, the eager flack noted that the Rangers goalie was a French-Canadian named Lorne Chabot. *Poof!* Just like that, Bruno changed his name to *Chabotski*. Suddenly, the Rangers goaltender was "Jewish," or at least in Bruno's fertile mind.

Now for an Italian. After perusing Lester's list, Bruno was mesmerized by a forward named Oliver Reinkka. The wheels were turning. Alas, an "Italian" name suddenly came to mind, and Oliver Reinkka turned into the much-needed "Italian" scorer, Ollie Rocco.

Most amazing of all is that throughout that 1926-27 NHL season, the New York papers listed the Blueshirts goalie as Lorne Chabotski and the forward as Ollie Rocco. (You can look up the box scores in *The New York Times* archives.) Yet when the Rangers visited hockey-smart Canadian cities such as Montreal, where Chabot was born, and Toronto, Lorne's name was as it should have been, Chabot; and Oliver reverted to Reinkka.

Johnny Bruno's Rangers ruse lasted for the season, but that was long enough. Within a year the Rangers had become the hockey darlings of Gotham, while the Amerks played second fiddle until they folded after the 1941-42 season.

83 | THE RED WING WHO "COULDN'T" SHOOT THE PUCK IN THE OCEAN

You've heard the expression dozens of times: "That no good so-and-so is such a bum forward, he couldn't shoot the puck in the ocean if he was standing on the shore."

But how many times has a victim of such a devastating hockey insult been able to prove—or disprove—the theory?

Well, once it actually happened.

The player in question was a Detroit Red Wings forward named Rene Fernand Gauthier, a native of Chicoutimi, Quebec, (home town of the immortal Georges Vezina). Gauthier had actually played some pretty good hockey during the World War II years with both the New York Rangers and Montreal Canadiens. But now the war ended, and the quality of the National Hockey League game experienced a steady rise. Concomitantly, Gauthier's game experienced an equally steady decline.

The more he skated for the Motor City sextet, the more difficult it was to imagine that he had once scored 14 goals for the Rangers and 18 for the Canadiens in a season. As a Red Wing, he was getting zilch.

In his first season with Detroit, he scored nine times and added three more in the playoffs. But a year after that, he managed only one, and the year after that only one again.

The less Gauthier scored, the more needling he absorbed, and the less ice time he was given. He was reduced to penalty killing—he was outstanding in that role—but he soon earned the label from his mates as the player who "couldn't put the puck in the ocean."

At the time, Stan Saplin was the publicity director of the Rangers and picked up on the Gauthier gag. "In no time at all," said Saplin, "the gag had spread around the league, but Fern took it good naturedly."

Another who heard the puck in ocean routine was Lew Walter, hockey writer for the *Detroit Times*. Eventually, the paths of Walter, Saplin, and Gauthier would cross, thereby creating a mini hockey legend.

"Lew got to thinking about all the ribbing," Saplin recalled, "but he realized it was unfair, in Detroit, to say that Fern couldn't put the puck in the ocean, since Detroit was hundreds and hundreds of miles from such a body of water.

"One morning, though, when the Red Wings checked into a New York hotel, prior to a game with the Rangers, Walter picked up a phone and arranged for a photographer to meet him. Then he phoned Gauthier and gave him specific instructions."

Saplin was informed of the grand scheme, as were a few New York writers. "Within an hour, Walter, the photographer, and Gauthier, carrying a hockey stick and a handful of pucks, were on their way downtown. They headed for the Battery, at the tip of Manhattan island, and there, with the photographer getting the evidence on film to disprove, once and for all, the false legend."

Just to be sure the evidence was well-weighted on Gauthier's side, a number of Detroit players were invited along to act as additional witnesses.

"We took along Gordie Howe, Ted Lindsay, and Marty Pavelich," said Walter. "They were able to refute the first two supposed 'misses' made by Gauthier."

One version had it that Gauthier missed on his first two attempts. "It was said," Walter laughed, "that as Fern shot the first puck, a seagull swooped down and snatched it—and then as the second puck went sailing out, a tugboat came by chuffing with a string of barges, on one of which the puck landed."

Both Saplin and Walter insist that Fern was able to shoot the puck into the Atlantic Ocean.

"Fern proved," Walter concluded, "not only that he could put the puck in the ocean, but also that he was a good sport by entering into the spirit of the rib. He was just a winger of great potential, of fine personality, and, if injuries had not hampered him, might have made him a true success in professional hockey!"

If nothing else, he will be remembered for his non-scoring; certainly a first in hockey.

84 | THE LINESMAN WHO NEVER FORGOT THAT HE WAS A HALL OF FAME HITTER

In some ways playing hockey is like riding a bike. Once you have the knack of it, the reflexes always remain there for use another time.

When it came to old-time body checking, few could match the thudding ability of Ivan "Ching" Johnson of the New York Rangers.

Over the years, the defenseman's' ability to use his hips as a moving hockey wall became legendary.

But eventually Johnson's years in the National Hockey League ended, and he became a linesman in the Eastern Hockey League. But deep down in the recesses of Johnson's mind, he retained the instinct for body contact and zest for action.

He displayed this one night while acting as a linesman for an Eastern Hockey League game at Uline Arena in Washington, D.C., between the New York Rovers and Washington Lions. Play flowed back and forth with great speed when, suddenly, a Washington forward sped free in a breakaway, pushing the puck ahead of his stick.

A witness described the episode that ensued: "Johnson suddenly forgot himself. For a split second he wasn't an official anymore; he was a Ranger defenseman all over again, and his goal was in danger. Johnson cut over in front of the fast-skating Lion forward and laid him low with a bodycheck that was as hard as any you'll ever see."

A newspaperman described the Johnson check in Promethean tones. "The check was so hard," said the reporter, "it felt like it made the Lincoln Memorial shake and quiver on its granite foundation."

Having returned to his senses, Johnson resumed his chores and later went into the Washington dressing room and apologized for his *faux pas*. "You know," he said, "I just can't explain it. Here was this guy racing for the goal and I just had to stop him. Why? Instinct, I guess. The old habit was too deep within me, and for a second I clean forgot where I was and what I was doing!"

85 | WHEN THE MOB NEARLY MAULED A GOALIE

When veteran hockey analysts look back on the "Good Old Days," they refer to the frontier style philosophy of the 1920s and 1930s.

No single episode better explains that raucous atmosphere than the near-assassination of a goaltender named Alex Connell.

So splendid was Connell as a puck-stopper that he eventually made it into the Hockey Hall of Fame. But at one point in Alex's life he almost was gunned down in the middle of Times Square.

It was in 1932 at the old Madison Square Garden on Eighth Avenue and Fiftieth Street in New York, and the Americans were hosting the Detroit Falcons in a game that would decide whether or not the Amerks would go into the playoffs later that spring. At the time, the Amerks were owned by the infamous Bill Dwyer, reputed mob boss, and undisputed King of the Bootleggers in New York as well as several other states.

The game was tied at the end of regulation time, 1-1, and the two teams went into a ten-minute overtime period. With about five minutes left in the period, Detroit received a penalty, giving the Amerks a much-needed advantage in manpower. New York players realized it was their opportunity to take the initiative and win the game. It was a must-win situation.

The red, white, and blue-clad Americans bore down and administered intense pressure on the Falcons. Red Dutton, then a battling defenseman for New York, took a blistering shot that, according to the goal judge, eluded Connell and ricocheted in and, just as quickly, out of the net. The red light went on, and the Amerks celebrated their "win." But trouble was brewing; the referee, George Mallinson, disallowed the goal. He claimed he had a perfect view of the play and the puck never went in. Connell agreed.

"The shot might have looked like a score to the goal judge, but the rubber definitely did not enter my net," recalled the erstwhile goalie.

During the melee that ensued, the goal judge berated the shocked goaltender with a string of the vilest profanities Connell had ever heard. Connell, being a man of dignity and pride, was not about to stand for any more of that kind of abuse. He skated around back of the net and, taking advantage of the man's nose, which was sticking through the mesh, bopped the goal judge directly and resoundingly on his protruding proboscis. This sent the surprised and infuriated goal judge reeling in his own blood, and started a panic among the security force at the Garden who knew the man to be a "high official in Bill Dwyer's mob."

Alex Connell had unknowingly put his own life in grave danger with one well-placed, ill-timed punch. But Connell was more concerned with the game, and after play resumed (the goal was not allowed), he held the Americans scoreless and the game ended in a 1-1 deadlock.

As Alex Connell left the ice, he noticed for the first time that there were policemen lining the walkway; that everywhere he looked he saw the boys in blue in great force blocking the spectators from approaching the players. When he got into the dressing room and began peeling off his sweaty uniform, two plain-clothed detectives walked up, identified themselves to him, and then stood on either side of him with their guns drawn.

It was then that Connell realized the seriousness of the actions he had taken. It was explained to him that the man he had punched out was Dwyer's right hand man, and that there might be some serious ramifications if proper precautions were not taken.

"Evidently," remembered Connell, "his finger on the red-light switch was as fast as the finger on his trigger."

Quickly, after he had finished dressing, Connell was shuffled into a waiting taxi and driven, along with his police escort, to the hotel where the team was staying. The cops combed the lobby for suspicious-looking characters before bringing in the befuddled Alex Connell. He was then given strict instructions not to leave his room for the remainder of the evening, and that he would probably be quite safe if he followed those words of caution without question. Needless to say, Connell was willing to obey, his fear and anxiety mounting with every cloak-and-dagger maneuver by the detectives.

Connell recalls how the rest of the evening went: "An old friend was visiting me that night, and after we had talked about the strange goings-on, we decided to leave the hotel to get some sandwiches before I went to bed."

"We went out the front door and had only walked about ten feet when I remembered the cop's warning. Then I noticed there were some people standing around us, one big mean-looking guy looked right at me and came towards us. We ducked into a diner and seated ourselves at separate counters. The large man came in and ordered me to go over to him for questioning. I paid no attention to him, so he repeated the order, adding that if I knew what was good for me I'd do what I was told.

"Then I walked over to him. He demanded, 'Aren't you Alex Connell, goalkeeper with the Detroit Falcons?' I replied that I not only did not know who Alex Connell was, but that I'd never heard of any Detroit Falcons.

"After a couple of minutes of him repeating the question and me repeating my answer, he apologized for bothering me and left."

The next day Connell learned that his quick thinking and fast talking had probably saved him from a one-way "ride" with the gun-slinging hoodlums.

"Years later, a New York newspaper man told me that the police had established the fact that both of the gangsters I had encountered that night had come to sudden endings. When I asked how, he said 'Bang! Bang!'"

86 | HOW A LIVE GOOSE VETOED A LIVE NHL PRESIDENT

As hard to believe—but true—stories go, this hockey tale tops them all. And when you find out how a live goose vetoed a live NHL president, you'll know the reason why.

For the most part, the presidency of the NHL has been a position surrounded by an aura of dignity. During the long reign of Frank Calder from 1917 to 1943, there was little levity associated with the NHL's highest office. The same might be said about the years following World War II, when Clarence Campbell, former referee, Rhodes scholar, and prosecutor at the Nuremberg war crimes trial, was the NHL president.

But in the sort period between the death of Frank Calder in 1943 and the nomination of Campbell in 1946, there was a rare lightheartedness combined with the office. The cause for the change was the personality of Mervyn "Red" Dutton, who was designated president following the death of Frank Calder.

Unlike Calder and Campbell, Dutton, who played and subsequently ran the New York Americans, was a rollicking type. His good-natured manner, the cockeyed behavior of the Americans, and the generally nutty world of hockey in New York in the 1930s had inured Red to frolicsome behavior. So, while he was league president, it was not surprising that he became the prime mover in an adventure that involved two newsmen and a very active piece of poultry named Mildred.

Mildred was a pure white goose with a distinctive beak that, in March 1943, accomplished what no player, manager, or owner could—she scared the living daylights out of the chief executives of the NHL and AHL in one night. The leading characters in what since has become known as "The Case of the Loose Goose" were Red Dutton; John Digby Chick, vice president of the AHL; and two Toronto sportswriters, Vern DeGeer and Jim Coleman. Oh, yes, and of course Mildred.

Dutton, an extrovert given to great bursts of enthusiasm, had promised to deliver a dozen ducks to his newspaper admirers after a hunting expedition in western Canada. "Red never delivered," said DeGeer, the late columnist for the *Montreal Gazette*, "so we needled him about the ducks whenever we saw him!" The goading of Dutton became more intense when the Stanley Cup semifinals series between the Toronto Maple Leafs and the Detroit Red Wings opened in Detroit on March 21. By the time the series switched to Toronto, the exasperated Dutton had decided to fulfill his promise.

"He smuggled a dead duck into my suitcase," DeGeer recalled. "When I got home and opened my valise, there was this terrible-looking bird that smelled to high heaven. I thought it was a funny sight, but my wife was madder than a hornet when she saw it. I knew it was Dutton's work, so I decided to get even." Accompanied by *Toronto Globe and Mail* sportswriter Jim Coleman, DeGeer went shopping for another duck at Wasserman's Poultry Market.

"I wish to buy a well-plucked duck," DeGeer advised Wasserman. "I'll tell you what I'm going to do," Wasserman replied. "I'm fresh out of well-plucked ducks, but as a special favor I'm going to let you have a goose. This is an exceptional goose, named Mildred, and I do not wish to kill her. Take her home, and she'll outtalk your wife!"

Aware that Dutton had checked into the Royal York Hotel, the writers decided to sneak Mildred into the president's suite. "We had Wasserman wrap Mildred up in paper," said DeGeer. Coleman than persuaded the assistant manager to give him the NHL's president room key. Meanwhile, Mildred remained silent in her wrapping. When Dutton arrived at the president's room, he deposited Mildred in the bathtub. He filled the tub with water, drew the shower curtain, and retreated with Coleman to a hiding place in the closet.

A few hours later, Dutton returned to freshen himself up for the third playoff game of the night. "I was half-naked when I walked into the bathroom," said Dutton. "As soon as I started shaving, I heard this strange hissing noise from the bathtub. I pulled aside the curtain, and this crazy goose flies at me and out of the room. I was dumbfounded at first, but then I went after it."

Out of the hotel room flew Mildred into the hallway, followed by Dutton, followed by Coleman and DeGeer. The incredible sight of a red-haired man, clad in only underwear, chasing a goose down the eleventh floor corridor at the Royal York Hotel, with two men alternately sprinting and howling in pursuit, proved too bewildering for a maid who was walking the other way.

"She became hysterical," DeGeer remembered. But, within a few minutes, DeGeer and Coleman were able to recover Mildred and this time carried her to the room of the late John Digby Chick, who was a portly gentleman who had left for the Stanley Cup match at the Maple Leaf Gardens. Once again, the writers placed Mildred in a bathtub, provided her with water, and drew the curtain to give her some privacy.

After the game had ended, John Chick indulged in a few drinks and returned to his hotel room. "After getting into his pajamas, he decided to have a nightcap," explained Coleman, "and he went to the bathroom to add some water to his drink." At the sink, Chick felt a pinching sensation on his right thigh, and as he looked down to observe what was pinching him, he saw Mildred leaning out from behind the shower. Dumbfounded, he glanced at the label on his bottle of alcohol to make sure he wasn't drugged.

Chick than picked up the phone and called downstairs, "Please send the house detective up to my room. There is a goose in my bathtub." The assistant manager got on the phone and urged Chick to "stay calm," saying, "Now, Mr. Chick, you just climb into bed and you'll find that the goose will be gone when you wake up in the morning."

The assistant manager's prescription failed to calm Chick down. "Either get rid of the goose or me," he demanded. "There'd be three house detectives up here if I had a girl in my bathtub. Get that man up here before I go out in the corridor and start screaming." Flanked by three house detectives, the assistant manager went up to Chick's room and, sure enough, found Mildred floating in the tub. She was removed, amid profuse apologies to Chick, and held in custody overnight at the hotel.

The following day, Mildred was punished for the trauma that she had influenced on the hockey executives. The assistant manager and the house detectives had Mildred for dinner—"But, not as a guest," said Coleman. "Chick and Dutton profanely declined an invitation to the banquet."

But Mildred managed to get even with her oppressors, even if she had to do it posthumously. "The assistant manager told me she was the toughest, worst-tasting goose he ever had," Coleman said. "But you couldn't beat her for laughs!"

87 | BY DOGSLED TO THE STANLEY CUP FINAL

Prior to 1917, any team could challenge to take home the Stanley Cup. In 1905, one of them just happened to be situated in the Klondike region of northwestern Canada. This was just a few years after the famed gold rush, and a number of wealthy miners from Dawson City decided that it was time the Klondike was represented in the Stanley Cup competition. A series of games was arranged, and the winning team carried off the Cup and held it until another challenger managed to win it.

So, the miners assembled a team and challenged the powerful Ottawa Silver Seven to a series in the Canadian capital. It was a bizarre idea from the beginning. For one thing, the Klondike team had to travel—mostly by dogsled—more than four thousand miles by the most primitive means of transportation.

And, for another thing, they had only one player, Lorne Hanna, who came close to passing for a major leaguer, by even the most remote standards. Undaunted, the boys from the northwest invaded Ottawa in January 1905, and, to no surprise to many, almost made a contest out of the first match. They ultimately were defeated 9-2, but it was enough to kindle hopes that the second match would be even closer, if not a triumph for the Klondikes.

But the bubble quickly burst with a deafening bang in the second game. The man responsible for defeating the visitors almost single-handedly was Frank McGee, the husky blond Ottawa center who many regard as one of the greatest players in hockey history, despite the fact that he played with only one good eye.

It took McGee seven full minutes before he gathered up steam, but once rolling he was unstoppable. One-eyed Frank scored two goals within 30 seconds and proceeded to go on a rampage that nearly mummified the Dawson City goaltender.

When it was all said and done and the game was over, McGee had scored fourteen goals, a Stanley Cup record that is virtually guaranteed to last as long as the NHL does. The final score? Ottawa 23, Dawson City 2.

88 | THE LIVE SKATING BEAR ON HOCKEY ICE

Of all the hockey promoters who have tried stunts to lure fans to the arena, none was more creative than Tommy Lockhart.

In addition to being business manager for the Rangers, Lockhart was also president of the Amateur Hockey Association of the United States. Then again, he also was president of the Eastern Amateur Hockey League and the New York Rovers, who played on Sunday afternoons in Madison Square Garden in the 1930s and 1940s.

One of Lockhart's challenges was to lure fans to Rovers games with various stunts. But by far the zaniest of all involved a live bear. Here's exactly what happened, in Lockhart's own words:

The bear was Jack Filman's idea. He was doing publicity for the Garden at the time and told me he'd seen this great act at a roller skating rink. I asked what the act was like, and he replied, "there's a bear that skates." I said, "How can he skate? And if he does, he's skating on a roller floor." Filman said, "Well, we can put him on ice skates, couldn't we?"

One discussion led to another, and we decided that maybe we could do something with it. So we went up to take a look at the bear. The bear's owner was a foreigner, and it must have taken eight hours for us to explain to him what we were trying to do and for him to say what his bear could do. He'd tell me the bear roller skates, and I'd tell him I'm not interested in roller skates, I want him to ice skate. If we'd say "skates" he would say he's got skates. Finally, he got the message.

We then asked how much he wanted, but before he could answer I said, "I'll give you twenty dollars," and he agreed.

With that settled, the next trick was to get the bear into the Garden before our Sunday afternoon doubleheader. I didn't want anybody at the Garden to know there was a bear coming in because there'd be hell to pay if they heard about it. It might start a ruckus, and there'd be eighteen guys wanting to know who's going to hold the bear.

After a while, I figured out the best technique. Early that Sunday morning, I went down to the employees' entrance on Forty-Ninth Street and talked to the guy at the door. I said, "there's a cab coming here with Jack Filman and a bear."

He says, "Wha?"

"I want you to let him in; open room 29 and get the bear in there. And don't talk about it."

Sure enough, Filman brings the bear, we lock him in Room 29, and then he and I put our heads together because we've got a big problem— where are we going to get skates for the bear? I mean, now we're dealing with a size-forty shoe. We went to the Rangers' equipment room, and the biggest skate we could find would only go as far as the bear's instep. Meantime, Harry Westerby, the Rangers' trainer, is screaming at us for taking his equipment for a bear. After we explained the act to him, he suddenly got enthusiastic and finally came up with the longest skate on the hockey team.

The next question was how to put the skates on the bear. By then, it was past noon, and everybody in the back of the Garden was getting into the act. The Met League game was starting and people were in the building, so we had to be sure the cops didn't let anybody through the back to disturb the bear. We had decided to attach the skates to the bear's feet with rope, which we did, making it pretty secure.

All of a sudden, the bear's owner chimes in that the bear can't go skating on the ice unless he goes out with him, and he's got to have skates too. The search is on again; we find skates, put them on the foreigner, and then learn he's never been on ice skates before in his life. He's even having trouble standing up in one place just in the room. While all this is going on, the bear is using the room as a toilet, and the cleanup crew had to come in with a pail and mop several times. It got so bad that the next day the Sanitation Department had to come in and disinfect the room.

Anyway, once we got a cord for the trainer to attach to the bear, we were about ready. I said, "Wait a minute, we ought to tell the two teams what we're up to." It was the Rovers against the Hershey Bears. I mentioned that the bear will come out and the trainer would be with him on skates, even though he couldn't skate. We had the thing perfectly timed out and an electrician had spotlights ready; I made the count-down: "Four, three, two, one!

We bring the bear out, with the guy holding the cord. He gets five feet, then ten feet out—and falls flat on his stomach. But he wouldn't let go of that cord, he just hung on as the bear skated all over the ice pulling him around the rink.

By this time the people were on their seats. I looked around and saw the General sitting there and enjoying it; everybody was having a great time. They were all howling, but now I knew we had another problem: how were we going to get the bear off the ice? That big fella was just skating all over the place with no intentions of leaving, and we had a hockey game to play. Already I had all kinds of advisors since the whole back-of-the-Garden crowd was in on this, but nobody could do a thing that worked. Finally, some woman walked up to me right out of the blue and said "You want the bear off the ice?" I replied, "Yeah, of course I want the bear off the ice!"

Next thing I know, she walks out onto the ice, no skates, no nothin', puts her two fingers into her mouth, whistles, and sure enough the bear comes over, pulling the Italian guy behind him like a car pulling a trailer.

We took the bear back to his dressing room, and along comes the General, who said he thought we had a helluva act. It was so good we took it down to Hershey, and it was a hit there too.

The bear eventually disappeared from view, but not Lockhart. After World War II, Tommy launched pro hockey on Long Island by helping build an arena in Commack, New York, which became the home of the Long Island Ducks.

By that time, Lockhart retired from the ice world, but his contributions never will be forgotten, zany or otherwise.

89 | IF THE NAME IS TOO LONG – CHANGE IT!

There may have been other NHL players with thirteen letters in their last name, but only Steve W-O-J-C-I-E-C-H-O-W-S-K-I of Fort William, Ontario, had his name changed so that writers and broadcasters could more easily pronounce and write it. Now, if you were Steve Wojciechowski, what would you change it to—Smith?

Well, Steve became Wochy. Back in the day, he played right wing for the Detroit Red Wings in 1944-45 and had a fair year with 19 goals and 20 assists, for 39 points in 49 games. Then World War II ended, and many players returned from service.

Steve played in the Red Wings' farm system, enjoying a brief NHL comeback in 1946-47. By that time, a lot of people could pronounce his name, but, alas, Steve failed to score again in the NHL. In five NHL games during his second time around, Wochy got exactly no goals, no assists, no points and no penalties. He did, however, thrive in the minors afterwards.

With Indianapolis, Philadelphia, and Cleveland, he continued to be a solid minor league player. Who knows how he might have starred if he had remained Wojciechowski!

90 | WHEN TWO WRONG GIACOMINS MAKE A RIGHT

As the saying goes, *Two wrongs don't make a right.*

In case of goaltender Ed Giacomin, it was a question of one wrong being right.

Or, to put it another way: which Giacomin was the right one—Eddie or his older brother Rollie.

Either way, in Sudbury, Ontario, the Brothers Giacomin both were goaltenders during an era when the minor (AA) Eastern Hockey League regularly fed top players to the American Hockey League and, occasionally, the National Hockey League.

In this case, Washington's entry in the EHL, the Lions, needed a second goaltender in 1958, and their coach Peanuts O'Flaherty had heard good things about Rollie Giacomin. He probably wouldn't have even considered Eddie because the latter was victim of an exploding kitchen stove that caused serious burns in his lower body. At one point it was believed that the younger goalie never would play hockey again; but he sure did.

Nevertheless, O'Flaherty summoned Rollie for an audition in Washington—but there was a hitch. Rollie's day job at an Ontario lumber mill would pay more than he'd be getting from the Lions and, besides, who said he'd make the team? With that in mind, the big brother asked the little brother goalie to stand in for him at Uline's Arena, home of the Lions.

O'Flaherty had not been advised of the Giacomin-for-Giacomin move until Eddie showed up, causing Peanuts to do a double-take. Miffed over the apparent double-cross, O'Flaherty scratched the replacement Giacomin for three games, each of which was lost by Washington. Finally, O'Flaherty figured he had nothing to lose and started Eddie Giacomin, who proceeded to win the next six games.

Eddie's audition was so successful that he arrested the attention of several AHL teams, and pretty soon Giacomin was starring for the Providence (Rhode Island) Reds, where his talent level soared to major league heights.

By 1965 several NHL teams eyed the youngster from Northern Ontario, but Rangers general manager Emile (The Cat) Francis beat them all to Giacomin. He offered Reds boss Lou Pieri four players including Marcel Paille, who had been the Rangers' number one netminder for Giacomin.

"Not only did I have to give up Paille," Francis often chuckled,

"but Pieri also demanded that I give him three other good-looking guys. He figured the women fans up there liked to watch handsome hockey players. So I did."

Francis never regretted the move. Giacomin became his protege and in 1987 was inducted into the Hockey Hall of Fame.

Ed Giacomin became a Hall of Famer by mistake. His older brother, Rollie, was supposed to try out for a minor league team, but sent Eddie instead. The kid brother was signed and made it to NHL stardom, while Rollie never got another tumble./AP Photo/John Lent

One can only wonder what might have been had Rollie Giacomin—and not Eddie—shown up in Peanuts O'Flaherty's office!

91 | "KILL THE REFEREE!"–THIS TIME IT NEARLY HAPPENED

rank Patrick, brother of Lester Patrick, co-patriarch of Hockey's Royal Family and known as "The Silver Fox," enjoyed just about every possible job one could earn in hockey.

A Hall of Fame member—as "builder"—Patrick also played the game and later was a coach and manager. He not only survived but excelled in every undertaking, including a stint as referee.

But one of those officiating undertakings almost led him to an undertaker. Yes, Frank Patrick was one referee who nearly died on the job.

This was in the pre-World War I, pre-National Hockey League days when the Federal League—not unlike baseball's version—was among the best in North America. Not surprisingly, the rivalries then were as heated as any contemporary Montreal Canadiens-Toronto Maple Leafs showdown or, in the New York-Metropolitan Area, between the New York Rangers and New Jersey Devils.

In 1906, no rivalry betrayed more ferocity than the animosity between supporters of Montreal and Cornwall, Ontario.

The latter was—give or take Toronto—the hockey capital of Canada, while Cornwall was a factory town which, as Patrick noted, "took its hockey seriously."

On the day that referee Patrick nearly was hung by fans, almost 3,000 fans squeezed themselves into the local arena built to hold about 1,800 spectators. In an interview with Canadian author Eric Whitehead, Frank described the melodramatic scene he entered.

"Walking onto the ice just before game time was like walking into a bear pit," Patrick remembered. "I knew that I had a nasty job on my hands. The Cornwall players wasted no time laying on the wood, and I immediately began assessing penalties against them in an attempt to control the contest."

He didn't.

Especially after Patrick penalized one of the home town boys "for opening a Montreal player's skull with his stick."

On the ensuing power play, Montreal scored, and the fans proceeded to go berserk and continued to do so after the game ended with Cornwall defeated, 1-0.

"When the game ended," Patrick remembered, "the crowd stormed down on to the ice and came after me. They had my route to the exit blocked, and I was all but surrounded. I don't believe that I would have gotten out of there alive had it not been for one of the Cornwall players."

Reddy McMillan, the Cornwall hero, refused to go along with the frenzied crowd and decided he had to protect the referee, whether the fans like his decision or not.

Patrick: "McMillan came to my rescue, flailing at the mob with his stick and screaming at them to get off the ice. He rushed over and backed me against the boards and stood in front of me while he tried to reason with the mob. He told them that to get me they'd have to get him first, and they finally backed off. Reddy saved my hide."

That wasn't the end of it. In those primitive hockey years it was customary for the referee to dress in the home team's room.

"I had some pretty anxious moments," Patrick concluded, "before I got out of the Cornwall quarters."

Some good came of the ordeal. Soon after Patrick's near-lynching, referees were granted their own separate dressing rooms!

92 | JAKE MILFORD—TRADED FOR TWO HOCKEY NETS

J ake Milford, general manager of the Los Angeles Kings, played minor league hockey in Springfield, Massachusetts, and he had some interesting experiences under the mercurial Eddie Shore.

Not the least unusual was him being traded for a couple of hockey nets! Milford recalled the incident in his own words: "Eddie called me in one day to tell me he'd sold me to Buffalo. As I stepped off the train, my eye caught a headline in a Buffalo newspaper—*MILFORD ACQUIRED FOR TWO HOCKEY NETS!*—I wasn't surprised.

"But Shore complained later that the Buffalo team had led him to believe they'd be *new* nets. Apparently the ones they had sent him were used."

Shore, therefore, retains the unique distinction of being the only owner to ever have traded one of his players for two nets and later to have complained that he's the one who got the bad part of the deal!

93 | THE WRONG METZ WON THE MOST CUPS

A fourteen-year member of the Toronto Maple Leafs, Nicholas J. (Handy Andy) Metz should have been the most acclaimed hockey-playing member of his family.

Otherwise known as "Red," Nick left his family's farm in Wilcox, Saskatchewan, to play for the Leafs beginning in 1934. He concluded it on a high note during the 1947-48 season, skating for the Leafs' Stanley Cup-winning club that President Conn Smythe dubbed "The best Leafs club ever."

Nick also made a name for himself as a premier penalty-killer along with Joe (Duke of Paducah) Klukay and was highly-regarded as both a defensive forward as well as a scorer. Yet, when all was said and done his kid brother, Donald Maurice Metz, spun a Hollywood-type hockey tale that to this day strains the credulity of ice historians.

Five years after Nick gained a slot on the Toronto varsity, Don made the big club but only for ten games in the 1939-40 season. He was returned to the minors and got another audition a year later, this time for 31 games. But the Maple Leafs' high command was not sufficiently impressed and returned him to the American League.

Don's yo-yo career now was in full motion. For the 1941-42 season, he played 25 games for the Leafs while honing his modest game to sharpness in the AHL once more.

Little was expected of Don as Toronto beat the Rangers four games to two in the Stanley Cup semi-finals to reach the Final against the Detroit Red Wings. Although coach Hap Day's club was favored to annex the second Cup in Leafs history, the Detroiters moved to the brink of a colossal upset. They won three straight and took a 2-0 lead in Game Four at Olympia Stadium in Detroit through nine minutes of the second period.

By this time, Smythe's general staff had made stunning lineup changes to reverse the tide of defeat that had enveloped the team with Don Metz, of all people, the centerpiece of all the moves.

To begin with, coach Day benched his leading scorer, Gordie Drillon—a future Hall of Famer—and replaced him with Don Metz. He also scratched his ace defenseman Wilfred (Bucko) McDonald and inserted a rookie Ernie Dickens while hoping for the best.

That would happen late in the second period of Game Four, when Toronto scored twice to tie the score. With eight minutes remaining, Don set up his big brother, Nick, for the winning goal. Don, himself, scored the winner in Game Five and totaled four goals and three assists as the Maple Leafs roared back to win four straight games and the Stanley Cup.

Try as he might, Don could not win a permanent job on the Toronto varsity but continued to star when promoted from the minors. A classic case was during the 1946-47 season, when the Leafs faced the favored Montreal Canadiens. During a collision, Metz bowled over the Habs' top center Elmer Lach, sidelining him for the Final series.

Montreal coach Dick Irvin accused Don of playing dirty and proclaimed that a Higher Authority was watching the series; if it was a clean check then Toronto would win, and if not it would be his Canadiens.

Not only did the Maple Leafs win the Cup, but the younger Metz brother finished the playoffs with a commendable two goals and three assists.

Ah, but even *that* is not the most remarkable thing about Don's career.

Throughout the history of Toronto's storied franchise, only three players have won five Stanley Cups. Two of them, goalie Walter (Turk) Broda and center Ted (Teeder) Kennedy, are Hall of Famers.

The third, Don Metz, *never played a full season with the team!*

94 | TAKING A BATH WITH TUBBY

A never-ending debate during the World War II years, when the Rangers held up the bottom of the NHL, was whether the New York skaters were that bad or whether goalie Ken "Tubby" McAuley was really the problem.

McAuley was in the New York nets on the night of January 23, 1944, the Rangers' night of infamy. With McAuley supposedly stopping the pucks, the Rangers were bombed, 15-0, by the Red Wings at Detroit's Olympia Stadium.

According to the Rangers coach at the time, Frank Boucher, the problem was less McAuley's than that of the inferior team in front of him. "Ken," said Boucher, "should have been awarded the Croix de Guerre if not the Victoria Cross for all the heroics he put up with in those years. Bless his heart, McAuley very rarely complained against the fates that had deposited him in our goal."

During the 1943-44 season, McAuley played in all 50 Ranger games, allowing 310 goals ("Only a fraction," said Boucher, "belonged to him; all of us should share in his glory.") for a 6.20 goals against average. He played 46 games the following season, this time trimming his average to 4.94. By 1945-46, the two Ranger regular goalies, Chuck Rayner and Jim Henry, were back from the war, and McAuley left the NHL for good.

95 | FIRED BECAUSE OF A HOT POKER HAND

During the early 1920s, it was not uncommon for one NHL team to "loan" a player or two to another club whose roster was decimated by injury. Once, the Montreal Canadiens "borrowed" a substitute player named Sam Goderre from Ottawa at the request of Canadiens' manager George Kennedy.

Two weeks later, Kennedy phoned Tommy Gorman, secretary of the Ottawa sextet, and pleaded with him to reclaim Goderre before the youngster was lynched by the Canadiens' players. "That kid" shouted Kennedy, "is a star poker player, *not* a star hockey player."

Sam eventually returned to Ottawa somewhat confused by the uproar he had ignited. Gorman was equally perplexed because he had known Goderre as a temperate young man not given to wild outbursts of gambling. "Now tell me, Sam," he asked the youngster, "what exactly happened with you and the Canadiens?"

What had happened was that the Montreal players were conducting a running poker game. When Goderre came along, he joined them and developed an amazing run of winning hands. "After two weeks," said Gorman, "he had practically cleaned out their wallets. That was the end of Sam's career with the Canadiens!"

96 | THE NEAR-KIDNAPPING OF A RANGERS STAR

When the Broadway Blueshirts made their National Hockey League debut in 1926, they were battling with the New York Americans, who already had spent a successful season playing at Madison Square Garden. Just how the Rangers could successfully compete with the Americans was a question that puzzled Johnny Bruno, who was sharing publicity chores for the Rangers.

It was Bruno's philosophy that something "big" had to be done to get the Rangers name in the papers before the home opener. What better plan than to have the club's superstar, Bill Cook, involved in a spectacular news story? Bruno knocked on the door of Rangers manager Lester Patrick.

"Come in."

"Mister Patrick, I have a terrific idea," Bruno declared. "Tomorrow, I will arrange to have Bill Cook kidnapped."

Before Patrick could summon his outrage, Bruno added: "But of course, we will locate him in time for him to make it to the game."

This time, the word blasted forth from Patrick's mouth.

"OUT! O-U-T. OUT!"

And with that suggestion, Bruno left.

97 | THERE WAS MAGIC IN LEONE'S BIG WINE BOTTLE

Over the decades, several teams have resorted to catalysts to enhance play.

For example, the Detroit Red Wings once employed an oxygen tank behind the bench. However, no team but the Rangers developed what became known as the "magic elixir."

A novice fan might find it hard to believe, but late in the 1950-51 season the hottest hockey items in New York City consisted of a strange liquid known as Leone's Magic Elixir and a *World-Telegram* sportswriter named Jim Burchard. During that season, life had become difficult for the Rangers.

Their record was well below .500 by early December 1950. Unless some sort of miracle could be produced, the future appeared bleak. Gene Leone, an affable restaurateur and ardent Rangers fan, pondered the ingredients in his kitchen one day, and suddenly an idea hit him. He'd distill some of his delectable juices, mix them with vintage wine from his cellar, and produce a "wonder drink" for the Rangers.

It would be good publicity for Leone, and perhaps it would boost his favorite team's sagging spirits. Just before Christmas, Leone perfected his formula and poured it into a large black bottle about three times the size of a normal pint of whiskey.

With appropriate fuss and fanfare, "Leone's Magic Elixir" was carried into the Rangers dressing room, where such heroes as Don "Bones" Raleigh, Pentti Lund, Frank Eddolls, and Neil Colville quaffed the brew. To say the results were amazing would be an understatement. They were hallucinatory. After drinking the elixir, the Rangers began to win and win and win. By early January, they had lost only two in a stretch of 11 games. But observers insisted the real test would come when the Blueshirts visited Toronto, where they hadn't had a victory for ages.

Now the fun started. Leone demanded that the magic elixir, whose formula was so secret that he wouldn't even trust it to paper, be prepared at the last possible moment. This was done on Saturday afternoon. When the brew was ready, he turned it over to Jim Burchard, who boarded a plane for Toronto. The plan was for Jim to arrive just before game time and present the potion to the Rangers.

Wearing his traditional black hat with its big brim turned down on each side, Burchard boarded the plane carrying a sealed bag containing the bottle of elixir surrounded by three hot-water bottles. A skull and crossbones adorned the black zippered bag. Unknown to the Rangers strategists, the Maple Leaf organization was arranging for the Canadian customs agent to seize the black bottle at Toronto Airport, denying its use to the New Yorkers.

"Naturally," wrote Al Nickleson in the *Toronto Globe and Mail*, "the Leafs had been hoping the flagon would have been seized as an enemy power when Burchard wouldn't explain its contents." But according to Nickleson, a *Globe* photographer named Harold Robinson saved the Rangers "by undermining the customs officer with stale jokes and Christmas cigars so that Burchard had no trouble slipping by."

Then Robinson pushed Burchard into his car and set several Ontario speed records driving to Maple Leaf Gardens just in time for the quaffing. Burchard had forgotten a corkscrew, so he had to push the cork down into the bottle. The Rangers, who actually detested the vile stuff, had their brief sips—some just gargled and spat it out—and then returned it to Burchard.

"When the cork stops disintegrating," explained Burchard as he poured what he couldn't drink down the sink, "we know that the stuff has lost its power. Why, look at that! Here comes a mouse up the drain waving a white flag." The Rangers, who enjoyed the joke more than the elixir itself, had their laughs and then went on the ice and performed like supermen. Within seven minutes of the first period, they had scored three goals and coasted to a 4-2 win.

Their victory caused a sensation.

"CAMERAMAN LUGS FLAGITIOUS FLAGON," screamed a headline in the *Globe and Mail*. "RANGERS NEW AID SCORNED BY LEAFS," the *Toronto Telegram* roared. While players and scientists speculated on the elixir's contents, Leone said he'd bottle the stuff and sell it commercially. "It tasted like the Atlantic Ocean," said photographer Robinson. "I think it's hot broth," said Leafs coach Joe Primeau. The Rangers had other opinions that are not fit to print, but the idea was appropriately conveyed by Toronto writer Bob Hesketh, who tasted the stuff. "It was a creamy liquid," said Hesketh, "that smelled just like water doesn't."

Occasionally, Leone would be distracted by business and forget to distill the potion. Once, when the Rangers lost to Detroit, Burchard explained, "The Leone brew wasn't on deck. Without it, the Rangers were under a psychological handicap." After the loss, an SOS was dispatched to Leone, who quickly prepared more of the liquid, and the Rangers whipped Toronto, 2-1, the next night. And so it went.

Two weeks later, Burchard arrived in Toronto without the bottle, and the Rangers lost. The papers attributed the loss to the missing elixir. Leone soon produced more, though, and it seemed to keep the Rangers in contention for a while longer. But the psychological value of the elixir had run its course, and the Blueshirts faded into fifth place at the end of the 1950-51 season.

The "elixir" that the Rangers really needed was in the form of good coaching and better players. Unfortunately, the New York sextet rarely obtained the formula.

98 | THE MOST UNUSUAL GOAL BY A GOALIE

Ever since R. F. Smith drew up the first rules for hockey in the late 1800s, it has been generally accepted that a goalie's place is in that abbreviated area between the posts. In fact, just about every man who has ever laced on the 40-pound leather pads has done his goaltending in close proximity to the cage.

There is, however, an exception to this, and the following brief story tells of a goalie who ranged with a rather spectacular result.

Chuck Rayner, who tended goal for the New York Rangers, harbored an obsessive desire to spring away from his nets, dipsy-doodle through the enemy's defense, and score a goal against his opposite number on the other side of the rink.

During World War II, Rayner's fantasy was realized. Playing for an All-Star Royal Canadian Army team, he was guarding the goal when a ten-man scramble developed behind his net. Suddenly, the puck squirted free and slid temptingly in the direction of the other goal.

What's more, there was nobody between Rayner and the puck. The bushy-browed goalie got the message, and with a five-stride head start on his pursuers, Rayner charged down the ice.

Chuck (Bonnie Prince Charlie) Rayner actually scored a goal on an end-to-end rush while playing for a Canadian Army team. But he never could do that as a New York Ranger goaltender./*AP Photo/John Rooney*

His opponents were so startled by the maneuver that they just stopped in their tracks to watch. What they saw was a phenomenon: Rayner skated to within firing distance and whacked the puck into the net! A goalie had scored a goal that looked as if he was a forward! The feat has never been duplicated in big-league hockey.

99 | HOW A LEAGUE PRESIDENT CREATED PHONY HOCKEY GAMES AND GOT AWAY WITH IT

om Lockhart, who is in the Hockey Hall of Fame, was one of the most fabulous characters in the ice game. One of his most significant contributions was the development of minor league hockey in the United States, and especially along the East Coast. Thus, the Eastern Amateur Hockey League was born in the early 1930s.

But in its first season, the EAHL had a problem: each team had a 48-game schedule, but there weren't enough dates available for all the contests. This was especially true for the teams that played in Madison Square Garden, which was bustling with other events.

What Lockhart did was make a deal with the teams in Baltimore, Atlantic City, Hershey, and even one in the Bronx.

What Lockhart did was arrange for the other New York-based teams to play their extra home games on the road. And Tommy gave each of those teams $250 to accommodate the metro area clubs. But Lockhart still had another dilemma: he still couldn't accommodate all of the extra games.

So, his solution was to make up games that didn't exist.

Here's how Lockhart explained it to me in a taped interview at his Manhattan apartment in December 1971:

"I had to cheat a little. I'd make up phony games; have the Crescents beating the New York A.C. 1-0 and put down somebody's name for scoring the goal and add an assist or two.

"Then, the next week I'd add two more and a couple of ties. Turned out 21 games were never played but nobody noticed it—at least no one in the league.

"One time a fellow from the *Times* got interested in the league and starting asking questions about those games. I said, 'Well I'll tell you. You know the Rangers play on Tuesday nights. The Americans play on Thursday night, and next week it's the reverse. I'd have the teams in there playing in the afternoons. We call them dark house games'

"If you look back in the *Times*, you'll find a story about Lockhart's 'dark house' games. The seats were standing up and cheering. But it actually happened—21 games never occurred, and the league finished its full schedule of games played in that first year."

100 | THE NAKED GOALIE WAS GRATTOONY

One of the most talented goaltenders of the expansion era was a French-Canadian lad named Gilles Gratton. In time, he would play for two World Hockey Association teams as well as the NHL's St. Louis Blues and New York Rangers. If nothing else, Gratton was eccentric; hence his nickname, Gratoony. Once during an interview, he told a reporter that one of his goals in life was to pose nude in *Playgirl Magazine*.

That never happened, but he did once take the ice during a practice attired only in his facemask. Next day's headlines proclaimed: "GRATTON, HOCKEY'S FIRST STREAKER."

"Big deal," said Gilles, recalling the episode. "Streaking was the fad at the time, so I did my thing and it got into the papers. At first the league fined me $10,000 because they thought I'd streaked in a game. I wouldn't have done it in a regular game because I knew I'd get thrown right out of the league."

101 | WHEN THE ABSOLUTELY PERFECT GOAL NET WASN'T SO PERFECT AFTER ALL

nvented prior to World War II, the "Art Ross Net" was deemed the official goal cage of the National Hockey League and it remained so through the early 1940s. In many ways it was perfect because its intricate design ensured that when a puck was shot into the twine it was virtually impossible for it to bounce out.

However, the Ross net had one "defect," so to speak. It was firmly affixed to the ice and was immovable no matter how hard it was hit by onrushing players. Eventually, it was deemed a hazard because players often crashed into it at high speeds and were injured by the stout, upright pipes which simply would not give in to the seemingly irresistible forces. Many players and managers agreed that something had to be done to ameliorate the hazard.

Enter Bert Lindsay, a former Hall of Fame goaltender—father of Hall of Fame left wing Ted Lindsay—who decided to invent an injury-proof net. And so he did.

The Lindsay net contained two hydraulic springs, similar to those on self-shutting doors. If a player crashed into the Lindsay net, the goal post tilted far back to absorb the blow and protect the player. Then, it would gradually return to its upright position when the player skated away unharmed.

Most of the hockey world greeted the Lindsay net with enthusiasm; that is, until it was pressed into action at Madison Square Garden during a game between the Rangers farm team, the New York Rovers and the Boston Olympics.

Players, fans, and hockey executives excitedly studied the results and, alas, there was one flaw. And a major one at that which had been overlooked by Bert Lindsay.

When goalies were under attack—say on a breakaway by an opposing player—the netminders developed a knack of deliberately leaning back on the collapsable Lindsay net, forcing it to bend backwards thereby cutting down the "angle" so that the sniper had less net to shoot at than normally. Thus, instead of a four-foot high by six-foot wide net at which to shoot, there was far less "air" for a sniper to find.

After too many goalies made it clear that they liked the push-back goal, the collapsable injury-proof Bert Lindsay net collapsed on its own merits.

Or, *de*-merits, as the case may be!